KU-753-786

Introduction

As the days grow longer and spring flowers burst through the ground, no one is as excited as we Norwegians. Hope is light green, as the Norwegian author Alexander Kjelland wrote: we survived another long, dark winter. A Norwegian will rest in winter and live through summer, and the level of energy changes drastically as the spring bursts, painting the beautiful nature a glorious light green. The Norwegian spring is generous when it finally comes. As a designer, I get to visit spring and summer on the screen in front of me through the dark winter months, while working with new fabric collections and books. The work is done with a feeling of longing that might just shine through.

In this book we have used the spring and summer collections Lemontree and Sunkiss. When designing these fabrics, my mind wandered to warmer climates and recalled childhood memories spending time at my grandparents' place in southern Europe, where the lemon trees thrived, the water was turquoise and the flowers were colourful. My grandparents are gone, but there is still a date palm left in their old garden named after me and planted the day I was born.

We hope you will find something to inspire you in this book, to get your house into a happy, colourful spring and summer mode. Many of the projects are suitable for children or grandchildren.

As always, I work with a team of wonderful people and I am so grateful for their talents. Seamstress Ingun Eldøy sews all the models and Linda Clements writes the explanations. Line Dammen works with styling and planning and Inger Marie Grini takes the wonderful pictures. I would also like to thank my publisher F&W Media for their fantastic cooperation.

Have a creative spring and summer!

Best regards

Return items to **any** Swindon Library by closing CGN
time on or before the date stamped. Only books
and Audio Books can be renewed - phone your
library or visit our website,
www.swindon.gov.uk/libraries

05/18

Central Library

01793 463238

→ HIG
21/05/18
CEN-EVE
19·09·18·
17·10·18

Copying recordings is illegal. All recorded items
are hired entirely at hirer's own risk

hine
ing

hanger

Hobbies

6 972 871 000

Contents

Lemonade Quilt

We are cutting lemons to make 'Lemonade' with this fun, modern quilt in bright Lemontree fabrics. The quilt uses all the fabrics from the collection, plus solid dove white for contrast.

MATERIALS

- Fabric 1: 2½yd (2.3m) – Solid dove white
- Fabric 2: ³/₈yd (40cm) – Lemontree yellow
- Fabric 3: ³/₈yd (40cm) – Lemonade yellow
- Fabric 4: ¼yd (25cm) – Hummingbird dove white
- Fabric 5: ³/₈yd (40cm) – Boogie Flower dove white
- Fabric 6: ³/₈yd (40cm) – Flowerfield yellow
- Fabric 7: ¼yd (25cm) – Flowerfield red
- Fabric 8: ³/₈yd (40cm) – Boogie Flower red
- Fabric 9: ¼yd (25cm) – Lemonade ginger
- Fabric 10: ¼yd (25cm) – Mosaics red
- Fabric 11: ³/₈yd (40cm) – Hummingbird coral
- Fabric 12: ³/₈yd (40cm) – Lemontree blue
- Fabric 13: ³/₈yd (40cm) – Lemonade blue
- Fabric 14: ¼yd (25cm) – Hummingbird blue
- Fabric 15: ³/₈yd (40cm) – Flowerfield blue
- Fabric 16: ¼yd (25cm) – Boogie Flower blue
- Fabric 17: ¼yd (25cm) – Boogie Flower green
- Fabric 18: ³/₈yd (40cm) – Hummingbird plum
- Fabric 19: ¼yd (25cm) – Mosaics green
- Fabric 20: ¼yd (25cm) – Lemontree plum
- Fabric 21: ¼yd (25cm) – Lemonade green
- Backing fabric 3½yd (3.25m)
- Wadding (batting) 61in x 80in (155cm x 203cm)
- Binding fabric ½yd (50cm) – Solid dove white
- Template plastic or thin card to make templates

FINISHED SIZE

52½in x 72in (133.3cm x 183cm)

Fig A

If you can't get hold of one or more of these fabrics, replace with fabric in similar colours

Fabric 1 Solid dove white

Fabric 2 Lemontree yellow

Fabric 3 Lemonade yellow

Fabric 4 Hummingbird dove white

Fabric 5 Boogie Flower dove white

Fabric 6 Flowerfield yellow

Fabric 7 Flowerfield red

Fabric 8 Boogie Flower red

Fabric 9 Lemonade ginger

Fabric 10 Mosaics red

Fabric 11 Hummingbird coral

Fabric 12 Lemontree blue

Fabric 13 Lemonade blue

Fabric 14 Hummingbird blue

Fabric 15 Flowerfield blue

Fabric 16 Boogie Flower blue

Fabric 17 Boogie Flower green

Fabric 18 Hummingbird plum

Fabric 19 Mosaics green

Fabric 20 Lemontree plum

Fabric 21 Lemonade green

PREPARATION AND CUTTING OUT

1 Before you start, refer to General Techniques: Making Quilts and Pillows. There are 240 blocks in the quilt, all made the same way. These blocks are assembled into two different units – Unit A and Unit B. Unit A is five blocks wide x seven blocks high, and this unit is repeated six times in the quilt. Unit B is five blocks wide x two blocks high, and is repeated three times at the bottom of the quilt. The fabrics used for the quilt are shown in **Fig A** and the quilt layout in **Fig B**.

Fig B
Quilt layout

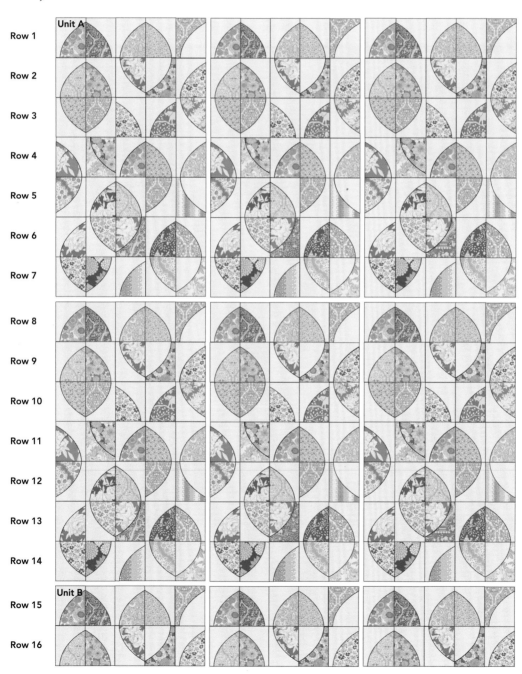

Row 1
Row 2
Row 3
Row 4
Row 5
Row 6
Row 7
Row 8
Row 9
Row 10
Row 11
Row 12
Row 13
Row 14
Row 15
Row 16

2 Each block is made up of two curved pieces, created from a pair of patterns. Two pairs of patterns are supplied (with seam allowances) – Patterns 1A and 1B face one way and Patterns 2A and 2B face the opposite way (see **Fig C**). Copy the patterns onto card or template plastic. Note: Some shapes in the quilt need to be cut with these patterns rotated 180 degrees.

3 Fig D shows how to cut the shapes. When cutting the shapes from the solid Fabric 1, the fabric is reversible, so cut the numbers of shapes stated and then rotate and/or reverse (flip) the shapes as necessary before use. Some of the print fabrics will need to be cut with all four patterns, to ensure that the shapes appear the correct way round.

For the concave shapes (Patterns 1A and 2A), cut the shapes from strips of fabric 5in (12.7cm) x width of fabric.

For the convex shapes (Patterns 1B and 2B), cut the shapes from strips of fabric 5in (12.7cm) x width of fabric. (The Pattern 1B and 2B heights are actually 4⅝in (11.8cm) but it will be easier to cut all fabric strips the same 5in (12.7cm) depth.)

4 You could cut the shapes as you go along, or cut the total numbers of 5in (12.7cm) x width of fabric strips needed. To cut all the strips needed, cut the following numbers of strips.

- From Fabric 1 cut seventeen 5in (12.7cm) x width of fabric strips.
- From Fabrics 4, 7, 9, 10, 14, 16, 17, 19, 20 and 21 cut one 5in (12.7cm) x width of fabric strip.
- From Fabrics 2, 3, 5, 6, 8, 11, 12, 13, 15, 18 cut two 5in (12.7cm) x width of fabric strips.

5 Beginning with Fabric 1, and referring carefully to **Fig E**, cut the shapes from the various fabrics in the numbers of pieces stated. Pay close attention to the way the shape is facing and use the patterns to cut the shapes. (Some of these shapes will be rotated later when you begin to piece the quilt.) **Fig F** shows the example of the pieces cut for the first block in the quilt (top left of quilt).

Fig C

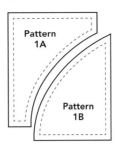
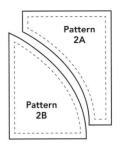

Note: Some shapes in the quilt need to be cut with these patterns rotated 180 degrees

Fig D
Cutting the pattern shapes

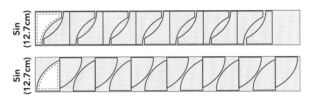

Fig E
Numbers indicate how many pieces to cut

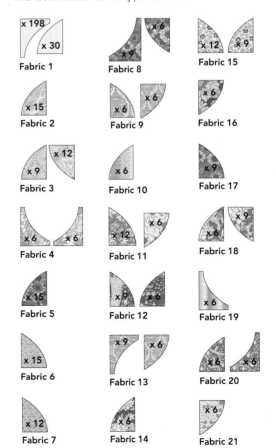

7

6 Cut the backing fabric in half across the width. Sew together along the long side and trim to a piece about 61in x 80in (155cm x 203cm).

7 From the binding fabric cut seven strips 2½in (6.4cm) x width of fabric. Sew together end to end and press seams open. Press in half along the length, wrong sides together.

SEWING THE BLOCKS INTO UNIT A

8 When all the block shapes are cut, begin to sew them together in blocks, as follows. Take the first two curved pieces (Fabric 1 and Fabric 5) and mark the halfway points along the curves by folding each piece in half and creasing or marking with a pencil (**Fig G1**). Pin the pieces right sides together, pinning first at each end and at the halfway points (**G2**). Add more pins along the curved edges, to match the curves exactly (**G3**). Now sew the shapes together using a ¼in (6mm) seam allowance. Sew slowly and follow the curve accurately. Snip into the curve slightly in places (**G4**). Press the seam to one side. Check the block is 4in x 5in (10.2cm x 12.7cm), trimming if needed (**G5**).

9 Repeat this process to sew the other curved units into blocks. Follow **Fig H** for the first row of Unit A, using the fabrics and shapes shown. Sew the row of five blocks together. Continue like this to sew the other six rows of Unit A. Press the seams of row 1, 3, 5 and 7 in one direction and the seams of the other rows in the opposite direction. Once the rows are made, sew them together and press (**Fig I**). Make another five of Unit A like this.

Fig F

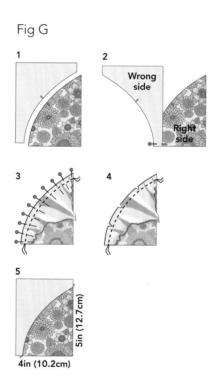

Fig G

Fig H

Numbers indicate fabrics (see Fig A)

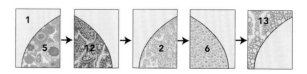

Fig I

Unit A – make
6 in total

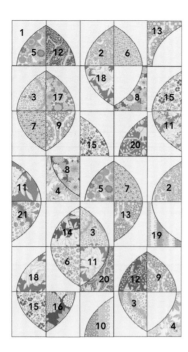

Fig J

Unit B
– make 3
in total

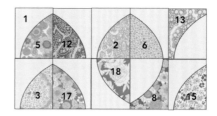

SEWING THE BLOCKS INTO UNIT B

10 Repeat this process to sew the blocks for Unit B, following **Fig J** for the fabrics and shapes. Make three of Unit B in total.

ASSEMBLING THE QUILT

11 When six of Unit A and three of Unit B have been made, sew them together in rows, as shown in **Fig B**, and press. Sew the rows together and press.

QUILTING AND FINISHING

12 Make a quilt sandwich of the backing fabric, wadding (batting) and quilt. Quilt as desired. Square up the quilt, trimming excess wadding and backing.

13 Use the prepared double-fold binding strip to bind your quilt (see General Techniques: Binding).

Lemontree Appliqué Cushion

This beautiful cushion has a lovely summery look. A turned-edge appliqué technique using paper patterns has been used.

MATERIALS

- Fabric 1: 1yd (1m) – Solid dove-white
- Print fabric scraps, maximum about 2½in x 5in (6.4cm x 12.7cm) of eleven print fabrics – see **Fig A** for the actual fabrics used
- Wadding (batting) 21in (53.3cm) square
- Thick, coated paper for appliqué shapes
- Paper piece glue
- Tweezers (optional)
- Cushion pad 18in (45.7cm) square
- Two buttons to secure back (optional)

FINISHED SIZE

19in (48.3cm) square

Fig A

Fabric 1
Solid dove white

Fabric 2
Lemontree yellow

Fabric 3
Lemonade yellow

Fabric 4
Flowerfield yellow

Fabric 5
Boogie Flower dove white

Fabric 6
Boogie Flower red

Fabric 7
Lemonade ginger

Fabric 8
Lemontree blue

Fabric 9
Lemonade blue

Fabric 10
Flowerfield blue

Fabric 11
Lemontree plum

Fabric 12
Mosaics green

MAKING THE CUSHION

1 The fabrics used are shown in **Fig A** but you could use your own fabric choices or a charm pack.

2 Cut Fabric 1 as follows.

- One piece 21in (53.3cm) square for the appliqué background.
- One piece 21in (53.3cm) square for lining when quilting.
- Two pieces 20in x 13½in (51cm x 34.3cm) for the back of cushion cover.

3 Fold the Fabric 1 appliqué background into quarters to lightly crease the halfway points. This will help you position the appliqués. The background is cut slightly larger to allow frayed edges to be trimmed later.

4 Prepare a master copy of the whole design by tracing or photocopying all the parts of the design given in the Patterns section and assembling them so you have a complete design. Place this behind the background fabric – you should be able to see the design through the fabric (**Fig B**). Pin in place.

5 The appliqué is worked using pre-cut paper shapes. Copy the individual pattern shapes onto thick, coated paper and cut out the shapes. Using a paper pattern, cut out a fabric shape ¼in (6mm) larger all round than the paper shape (**Fig C**). Snip notches in the edge of the fabric. Spread a little glue along the edge of the paper and fold the fabric seam allowance over the paper shape (**Fig D**). Work all round the shape in this way and then press. Prepare all shapes this way.

6 Place the appliqués on the background fabric as shown in **Fig E** – the paper design underneath will help with the placement of the pieces. Use a little glue to stick all the shapes in place, or use pins or tacking (basting) stitches. Remove the large paper pattern. Now sew the appliqués to the fabric with tiny stitches around the edges, matching the sewing thread to the fabric. Try not to sew through the paper. When the shapes are sewn in place remove the paper shapes. From the back of the background fabric cut through the fabric *only* behind each appliqué and coax out the paper. Use tweezers if needed. Press the work. If the cut-up edges on the back don't sit smoothly, fix to the middle of the appliqué with a little glue.

7 Make a quilt sandwich of the patchwork, wadding (batting) and lining fabric. Quilt as desired. Trim the work down to 20in (51cm) square.

8 The cushion is assembled with an overlapped back. Use the two pieces of Fabric 1 and follow the instructions in General Techniques: Cushion Cover. Use buttons to secure the back if you wish.

Fig B

Paper design behind background fabric

Fig C   **Fig D**

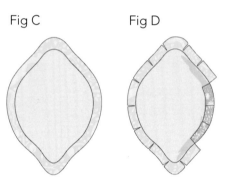

Fig E

Cushion layout – numbers indicate fabrics used (see Fig A)

Patch Cats

These cute cats would make a wonderful gift. Specific fabrics and instructions are given for the blue cat, but you could just choose any four print fabrics plus the solid dove white. The fabric amounts allowed are generous.

MATERIALS

- Fabric 1: one fat quarter – Solid dove white
- Fabric 2: one fat quarter – Lemonade green
- Fabric 3: one fat quarter – Flowerfield blue
- Fabric 4: one fat quarter – Boogie Flower blue
- Fabric 5: 18in x 27in (46cm x 68.5cm) – Boogie Flower dove white
- Toy stuffing (fibre fill)
- Black hobby paint and a big ball-headed pin or thin brush for eyes
- Lipstick or rouge and a dry brush for rosy cheeks
- Embroidery cotton (floss) for stitching nose

FINISHED SIZE

24in (61cm) tall

Fig A

If you can't get hold of one or more of these fabrics, replace with fabrics in similar colours

 Fabric 1 Solid dove white

 Fabric 4 Boogie Flower blue

 Fabric 2 Lemonade green

 Fabric 5 Boogie Flower dove white

 Fabric 3 Flowerfield blue

MAKING THE CAT

1 Before you start, refer to the notes in General Techniques: Making Softies. Copy the pattern pieces from the Patterns section and cut out the shapes. Some patterns are in parts to fit the page, so assemble as needed. **Fig A** shows the fabrics used.

2 Head: For the face, fold Fabric 1 in half, right sides together. Mark and cut out two mirrored face shapes with a seam allowance all round. Mark the small lines on the fabric edge where shown on the pattern. (Ensure you leave enough fabric to cut the eye patch.)

3 Mark the eye patch circle on the folded dove white fabric. Sew all around the circle and cut out with a seam allowance. Cut a slit on one fabric layer and turn through to the right side. Press and set aside.

4 For the head front and back pieces, cut a piece of Fabric 3 and Fabric 4 each 14in x 9in (35.6cm x 23cm). Place right sides together with Fabric 3 on top. Mark and cut out with a seam allowance all round.

5 Sewing each side of the head in turn, pin a dove white face piece right sides together with a Fabric 4 head front piece, matching up the small marks first and then easing the rest of the curves to fit together (**Fig B1**). Sew the curved seam and press the seam open. Repeat with the other side of the face (**B2**). Sew the two front head pieces together, down along the nose and along the chin (**B3**).

6 Pin the two head back pieces right sides together. Sew down the centre join, leaving a gap, as on the pattern (**Fig C1**). Pin the head front and head back pieces together, matching seams, and sew all around the edge (**C2**). Turn through to the right side through the gap and press. Stuff the head and sew up the gap.

7 Arms and Legs: The arms and legs are cut out from pieced fabrics, so the paws and feet are in a different fabric to the main arm and leg pieces. The fabric order is reversed on the back of the limbs. From Fabric 3 and Fabric 4 cut a piece about 14in x 10½in (35.6cm x 26.7cm). From Fabric 2 and Fabric 5 cut a piece about 14in x 4in (35.6cm x 10.2cm). Sew the larger piece of Fabric 4 to the smaller piece of Fabric 2 and press. Sew the larger piece of Fabric 3 to the smaller piece of Fabric 5 and press (**Fig D1**).

8 Place the Fabric 4+2 piece right side down on the Fabric 3+5 piece, aligning the sewn seams. Place the leg and arm patterns as shown in **Fig D2**, placing the dashed line of the paw/foot horizontally on the seamline. Draw around the patterns, allowing space for seam allowances. Sew on the solid line of each of the patterns. Cut out each shape with a seam allowance. Turn the limbs through to the right side and stuff.

9 Body: The patchwork body is created in a similar way to the limbs, except only two pieces of fabric are needed as the front and back body pieces are the same fabric. From Fabric 2 cut a piece about 14in x 5½in (35.6cm x 14cm). From Fabric 5 cut a piece about 14in x 7in (35.6cm x 18cm). Sew the pieces together along the long side and press open.

Fig B

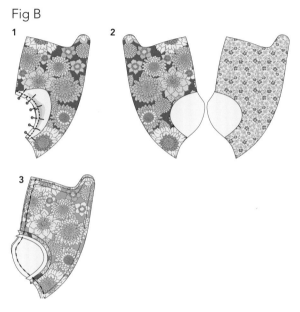

Fig C

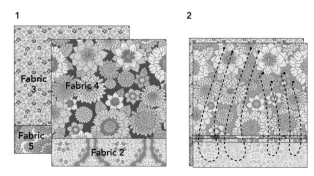

Fig D

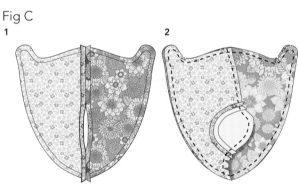

10 Fold the pieced fabric in half, right sides together. Mark the pattern, placing the dashed line of the pattern horizontally on the seamline. Sew along the marked sewing lines (**Fig E1**). Cut out with a seam allowance all round (**E2**). Turn up and press the hem at the bottom of the body (**E3**). Keep wrong side out and don't stuff yet.

11 Tail: For the tail take the remaining piece of Fabric 5 and fold it in half vertically, right sides together. Mark the tail pattern, sew and cut out with a seam allowance. Turn through to the right side, press and stuff.

ASSEMBLING AND FINISHING
12 Place the stuffed arms inside the body and sew securely in place (**Fig F1**). Turn the body through to the right side and stuff. Before closing the bottom seam, pin the legs in position towards the sides of the gap and pin the tail in the centre of the opening. Hand sew securely into place (**F2**).

Fig E

1

Fold

2

3

Turn up and press hem

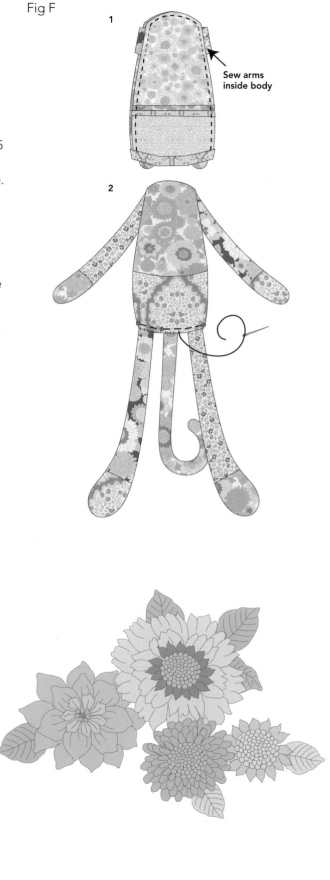

Fig F

1

Sew arms
inside body

2

13 Position the circular eye patch on one side of the face and sew it into place with tiny stitches and matching thread.

14 Hand sew the base of the head to the top of the body. To make the face, use black hobby paint for the eyes and a little lipstick or rouge for the cheeks. Use a big ball-headed pin to mark where the eyes will be and wiggle the pin back and forth to make a hole. Dip the head of the pin in paint and stamp eyes (**Fig G**). Alternatively, find something else to use as a stamp, or draw circles about ¼in (6mm) in diameter, and paint on eyes with a thin brush. Once the eyes are dry, mark rosy cheeks with lipstick or rouge and a dry brush. Finally, satin stitch the nose with the pink embroidery thread.

Fig G

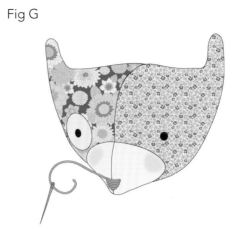

Patchwork Lemons

These lemons are really easy to sew and make attractive decorations. They use fabrics from the Lemontree range and you could make a luscious bowlful using different fabric combinations.

MATERIALS

- Two different print fabrics for the lemon, each about 8in (20.3cm) square
- One print fabric for the leaf, about 5in (12.7cm) square
- Toy stuffing (fibre fill)
- Short piece of string

FINISHED SIZE

4in (10.2cm) tall

MAKING A LEMON

1 Before you start, refer to the notes in General Techniques: Making Softies. Copy the patterns onto thick paper and cut out the shapes.

2 Place the fabric squares for the lemon right sides together and draw the lemon pattern twice. Add a ¼in (6mm) seam allowance all round (**Fig A**) and then cut out the shapes. You now have four lemon pieces.

Fig A

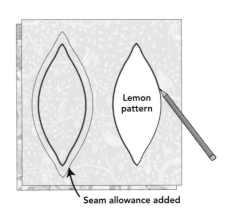

Lemon pattern

Seam allowance added

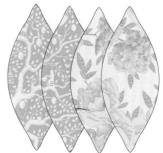

Fig B

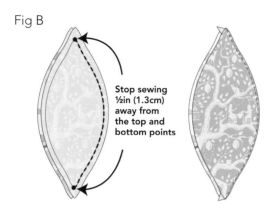

Stop sewing ½in (1.3cm) away from the top and bottom points

4 To make the leaf, fold the fabric for the leaf right sides together, draw the pattern and sew (**Fig D**). Leave an opening for turning in the seam. Cut out with a seam allowance all round, leaving a slightly bigger allowance around the gap. Turn through to the right side, sew the gap shut and press.

5 To finish, cut a piece of string, double it to make a loop and tie a knot in the end. Trim off the end pieces. Sew the knot to the top of the lemon and then sew the leaf onto the knot.

Fig C

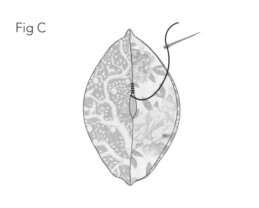

Fig D

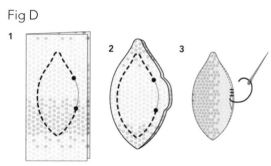

3 To sew the lemon together take two sections, one of each fabric. Place them right sides together. With a pencil, mark a dot ½in (1.3cm) away from the top and bottom points. Sew a ¼in (6mm) seam down the long side, starting and stopping at these marked points (**Fig B**). Backstitch for a few stitches at the start and finish of the seam to secure the stitching. Turn to the right side and press. Repeat this with the other pair. Now sew the two pairs together in the same way. Sew the final seam, leaving an opening for turning. Turn through, stuff and then sew the opening shut (**Fig C**).

Scrap Bowls

These handy bowls are ideal for so many things and are perfect for using up scraps of fabric. Make as many as you like in different sizes – they're great for gifts too.

MATERIALS

- Variety of fabrics cut into long strips about 1in–1¼in (2.5cm–3.2cm) wide
- Rope or thick cord, about ⅜in (1cm) in diameter
- Strong scissors
- Adhesive tape
- Suitable ceramic or plastic bowl to act as a mould
- Hot glue gun (optional)

FINISHED SIZE

Final size depends on the bowl you have used as a mould

MAKING A BOWL

1 Choose a bowl in the size you want and place it upside down on the table. Starting at the bottom of the bowl, measure around the bowl with the rope and make a mark to show where to cut the rope. Tape around the rope on each side of the mark and then cut the rope (**Fig A**). Form the rope into a circle and tape the two ends together. Place the circle on the bowl. Continue like this, measuring and making circles until you have covered the sides of the bowl (**Fig B**). The bottom of the fabric bowl will be made at the end without using the bowl.

Fig A

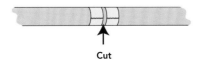

Cut

Fig B

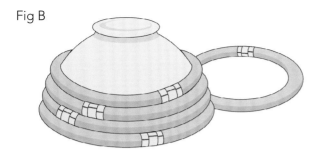

2 Lift the rope circles off the bowl. Keep track of the order of the circles, as some can be very similar in size. Begin with the largest circle. Start to the left of the taped area so that the first strip will cover the join in the rope. Fold in about one third of the side of the fabric strip and start wrapping the strip tightly around the rope, angling it so it covers the rope in a slanted angle (**Fig C**). Fold in the fabric edge as you go and make sure you always overlap the raw edge from the last round. At the end of the strip pull it tight against the rope and secure with a pin while you get the next strip ready (**Fig D**).

3 Pull out the pin and while holding the tip in place, place the end of the new strip on top and secure with the pin. Wrap the first round slanted a little backwards to cover the join, pulling out the pin before you continue. When the whole circle is almost covered, fold in the other side of the fabric strip (**Fig E**). Wrap two or three times to cover gap well.

Fig C

Fig D

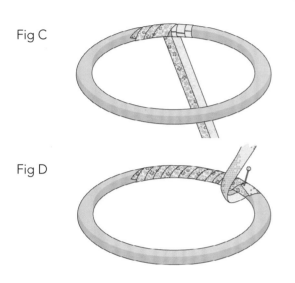

4 Cut off the strip and fold in the tip. Secure it with a pin and tack (baste) it in place (**Fig F**). If possible try to have the sewn end on the underside of the circle on the finished bowl. Repeat this fabric wrapping on all of the rope rings.

5 Reconstruct the fabric bowl by placing the covered rings back on the bowl. Secure together by sticking pins through the rope layers and then lift the fabric bowl off the bowl. Place it bottom down on the table.

Fig E

Fig F

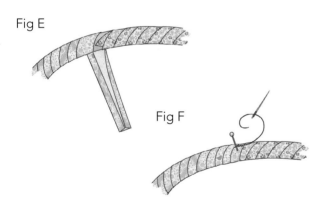

6 To make the bottom, place the rope inside the fabric bowl and create a circle in the bottom. Mark it and make a circle as you did before. Place it back in the bottom of the bowl, and then create a smaller circle to go inside the first. Continue until the opening left is too small to make a circle. Cover this final gap by creating a U-shaped piece with the rope (**Fig G**). Cover the circles and the U-shaped piece as described above and then press everything down inside the bottom of the bowl.

Fig G

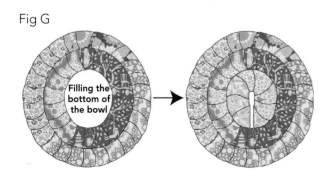

Filling the bottom of the bowl

7 To assemble the bowl, you can hand sew the rings together by sewing from the inside to the outside and back, catching the top ring and the bottom ring every other time, but this is a long job. It is quicker and easier to use a small hot glue gun to fix the rings together, as follows. Start at the top, lift an area of the top ring, add a bit of glue and press together. Glue the top ring in place area by area before continuing to the next. Remove pins as you go. When the bowl shape is glued together lift out the bottom pieces. Put a bit of glue around the outside of the biggest bottom ring and quickly press it in place. Continue like this until all rings and the U shape are fixed in place.

Whale Quilt

Make this fun summer quilt of patchwork whales using fabrics from the Sunkiss collection plus three Medium Dots fabrics. A warm sand solid fabric is used for a contrast background. The making requires some concentration and following the diagrams and instructions carefully. Instead of long ⅛yd cuts of fabric you could buy fat eighths 10½in x 18in (26.7cm x 46cm).

MATERIALS

- Fabric 1: 1⅝yd (1.5m) – Solid warm sand
- Fabric 2: ¼yd (25cm) – Imogen teal
- Fabric 3: ⅛yd (15cm) – Suraj teal
- Fabric 4: ⅛yd (15cm) – Beach Peony teal
- Fabric 5: ⅛yd (15cm) – Ocean Flower teal
- Fabric 6: ¼yd (25cm) – Charlotte teal
- Fabric 7: ⅛yd (15cm) – Beach Peony blue
- Fabric 8: ⅛yd (15cm) – Charlotte blue
- Fabric 9: ½yd (50cm) – Grandma's Rose blue, for binding
- Fabric 10: ¼yd (25cm) – Imogen blue
- Fabric 11: ⅛yd (15cm) – Ocean Flower blue
- Fabric 12: ⅛yd (15cm) – Imogen pink
- Fabric 13: ¼yd (25cm) – Beach Peony ginger
- Fabric 14: ⅛yd (15cm) – Charlotte ginger
- Fabric 15: ⅛yd (15cm) – Suraj lilac
- Fabric 16: ⅛yd (15cm) – Grandma's Rose lilac
- Fabric 17: ¼yd (25cm) – Beach Peony lime
- Fabric 18: ⅛yd (15cm) – Imogen green
- Fabric 19: ¼yd (25cm) – Grandma's Rose pink
- Fabric 20: ¼yd (25cm) – Ocean Flower pink
- Fabric 21: ¼yd (25cm) – Charlotte pink
- Fabric 22: ¼yd (25cm) – Medium Dots teal
- Fabric 23: ⅛yd (15cm) – Medium Dots blue
- Fabric 24: ¼yd (25cm) – Medium Dots pink
- Backing fabric 3¼yd (3m)
- Wadding (batting) 58½in x 70in (149cm x 178cm)
- Removable fabric marker
- Six ¾in (20mm) diameter buttons for whale eyes – one pack of Tilda buttons has two each of Boogie Flower red (100010), Boogie Flower blue (100011) and Boogie Flower dove white (100009)

FINISHED SIZE

50in x 61in (127cm x 155cm)

Fig A

If you can't get hold of one or more of these fabrics, replace with fabric in similar colours

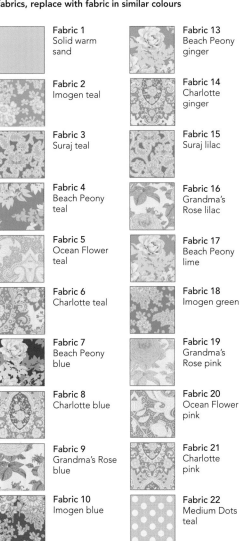

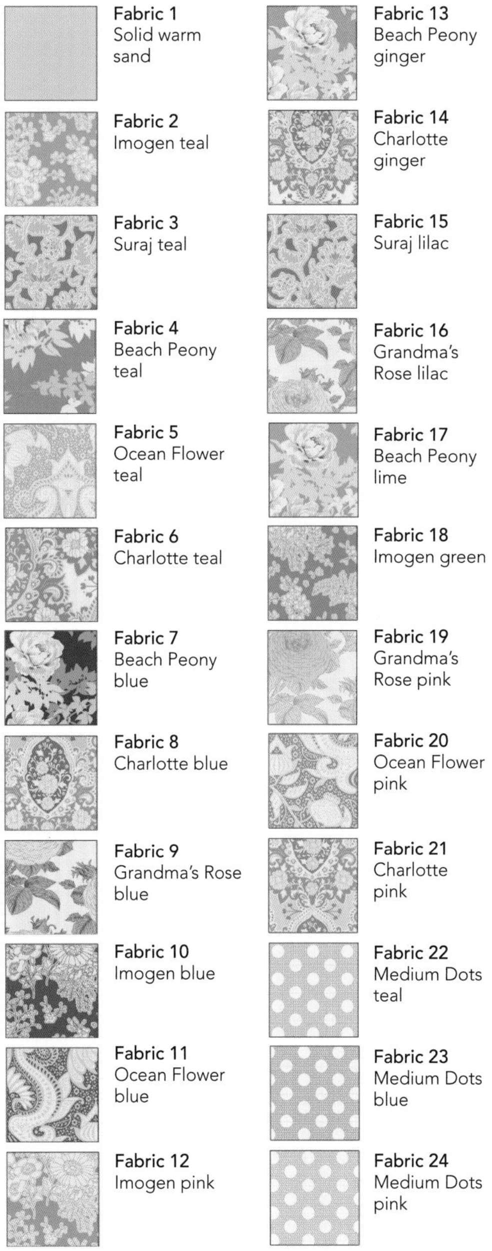

Fabric 1 Solid warm sand

Fabric 2 Imogen teal

Fabric 3 Suraj teal

Fabric 4 Beach Peony teal

Fabric 5 Ocean Flower teal

Fabric 6 Charlotte teal

Fabric 7 Beach Peony blue

Fabric 8 Charlotte blue

Fabric 9 Grandma's Rose blue

Fabric 10 Imogen blue

Fabric 11 Ocean Flower blue

Fabric 12 Imogen pink

Fabric 13 Beach Peony ginger

Fabric 14 Charlotte ginger

Fabric 15 Suraj lilac

Fabric 16 Grandma's Rose lilac

Fabric 17 Beach Peony lime

Fabric 18 Imogen green

Fabric 19 Grandma's Rose pink

Fabric 20 Ocean Flower pink

Fabric 21 Charlotte pink

Fabric 22 Medium Dots teal

Fabric 23 Medium Dots blue

Fabric 24 Medium Dots pink

PREPARATION

1 Before you start, refer to General Techniques: Making Quilts and Pillows. In the quilt there are six Whale blocks (in four different colourways) and six Partial Whale blocks (in four different colourways). The fabrics used for the quilt are shown in **Fig A** and the quilt layout in **Fig B**. Each block is made up of many pieces, so the cutting out is described for a Whale block (steps 2 and 3) and a Partial Whale block (step 16). Note that the whales reverse direction in alternate rows of the quilt. The shape of the whale is achieved by sewing shapes of solid Fabric 1 to print shapes. Sometimes these Fabric 1 pieces are squares, but sometimes they are rectangles. Two different techniques (described later) are needed to achieve these triangle corners.

CUTTING OUT FOR A WHALE BLOCK

2 Each full Whale block is made up of nine units – see **Fig C** for how these units go together, and **Fig D** identifying the individual pieces. The cutting out and making of Whale block 1 is described in detail. You will find it easier to keep track of all of the pieces if you cut the pieces for one unit at a time and make the unit before moving on to the next one.

3 For one Whale block 1 cut the following pieces (¼in/6mm seam allowances are included) – see **Fig D**.

Unit 1
a 2½in x 7½in (6.4cm x 19cm) in Fabric 10.
b 2½in x 2¾in (6.4cm x 7cm) in Fabric 1.
c 2½in x 1in (6.4cm x 2.5cm) in Fabric 1.
d 2½in x 8in (6.4cm x 20.3cm) in Fabric 6.

Fig B
Quilt layout

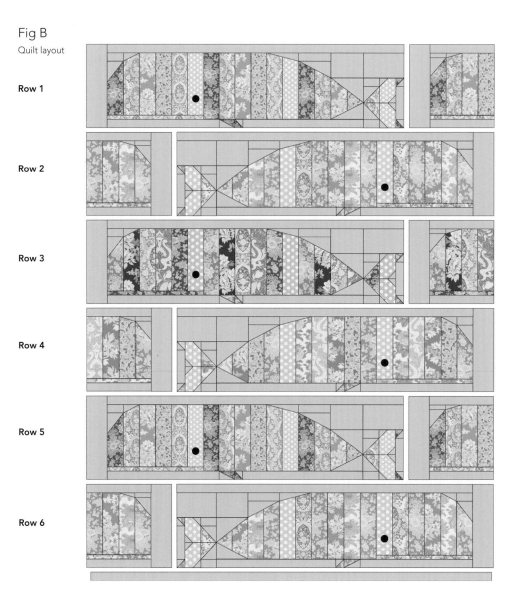

Row 1

Row 2

Row 3

Row 4

Row 5

Row 6

e 2½in x 1in (6.4cm x 2.5cm) in Fabric 1.
f 2½in x 8in (6.4cm x 20.3cm) in Fabric 17.
g 2½in x 8in (6.4cm x 20.3cm) in Fabric 3.
h 2½in x 8in (6.4cm x 20.3cm) in Fabric 21.
i 2½in x 8in (6.4cm x 20.3cm) in Fabric 22.
j 12½in x 1in (31.8cm x 2.5cm) in Fabric 21.

Unit 2
a 2½in x 8½in (6.4cm x 21.6cm) in Fabric 10.
b 2½in x 8½in (6.4cm x 21.6cm) in Fabric 6.
c 2½in x 8½in (6.4cm x 21.6cm) in Fabric 17.
d 2½in x 8½in (6.4cm x 21.6cm) in Fabric 3.

Unit 3
a 2½in x 8½in (6.4cm x 21.6cm) in Fabric 21.
b 2½in x 8½in (6.4cm x 21.6cm) in Fabric 22.
c 4½in x 1½in (11.4cm x 3.8cm) in Fabric 1.

Unit 4
a 2½in x 7½in (6.4cm x 19cm) in Fabric 10.
b 2½in x 7½in (6.4cm x 19cm) in Fabric 6.
c 4½in x 2½in (11.4cm x 6.4cm) in Fabric 1.
d 4½in x 1½in (11.4cm x 3.8cm) in Fabric 1.

Unit 5
a 2½in x 5½in (6.4cm x 14cm) in Fabric 17.
b 2½in x 5½in (6.4cm x 14cm) in Fabric 3.
c 4½in x 2½in (11.4cm x 6.4cm) in Fabric 1.
d 4½in x 3½in (11.4cm x 9cm) in Fabric 1.
e 4½in x 3½in (11.4cm x 9cm) in Fabric 1.

Unit 6
a 14½in x 1½in (36.8cm x 3.8cm) in Fabric 1.
b 3in x 1⅞in (7.6cm x 4.8cm) in Fabric 1. Cut into two triangles. (These triangles are cut larger, so they can be pieced later.)
c 3in x 1⅞in (7.6cm x 4.8cm) in Fabric 10. Cut into two triangles.
d 2in (5cm) square in Fabric 10. Cut into two triangles.
e 2in (5cm) square in Fabric 1. Cut into two triangles.
f 15½in x 1½in (39.4cm x 3.8cm) in Fabric 1.

Unit 7
a Two pieces 2½in x 1½in (6.4cm x 3.8cm) in Fabric 1.
b 3in (7.6cm) square in Fabric 1. Cut into two triangles. (These triangles are cut larger, to be pieced later.)
c 3in (7.6cm) square in Fabric 21. Cut into two triangles.
d Two pieces 2½in x 3½in (6.4cm x 9cm) in Fabric 22.
e Four 1½in (3.8cm) squares in Fabric 1.
f Two 1⅞in (4.8cm) squares in Fabric 10. Cut each square into two triangles.

g Two 1⅞in (4.8cm) squares in Fabric 1. Cut each square into two triangles.
h 1½in x 4½in (3.8cm x 11.4cm) in Fabric 1.
i 5½in x 3½in (14cm x 9cm) in Fabric 1.

Unit 8 – One 37½in x 1½in (95.3cm x 3.8cm) in Fabric 1.

Unit 9 – One 3in x 10½in (7.6cm x 26.7cm) in Fabric 1.

Fig C
Whale block 1

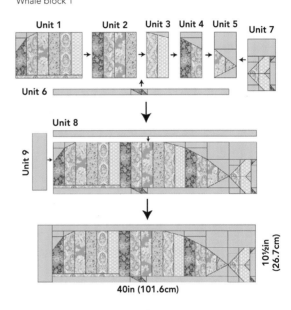

Fig D
Letters indicate fabric cut sizes (see step 3)

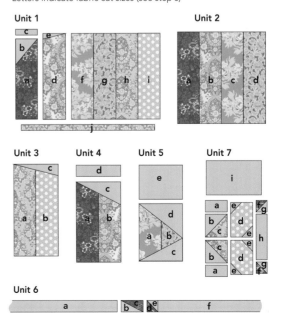

MAKING A WHALE BLOCK 1

4 To piece Whale block 1, work on each unit separately. Press seams open or to one side.

Sewing Unit 1: Lay out the correct fabric pieces as shown in **Fig D**. Sew pieces **f**, **g**, **h** and **i** together along their long sides. For piece **a** and **b** follow the instructions below on Creating a Rectangle Triangle on Corners. Once the triangle corner is created sew piece **c** on top. Use the same technique for pieces **d** and **e**. Sew **a/b/c** to **d/e** and then sew to **f/g/h/i**. Add piece **j** to the bottom to finish Unit 1.

5 Creating a Rectangle Triangle on Corners: It is important to place the rectangle correctly before sewing, so when the unit is sewn to another unit later, the point of the triangle will end up exactly in the top corner of the unit. **Fig E** shows how to achieve this with Unit 1, pieces **a** and **b**. Use a removable marker to mark a ¼in (6mm) seam allowance on the *right* side of piece **a** (shown in red). Now take rectangle **b** and mark the seam allowance on the *wrong* side of the fabric (**E1**). Draw a line (shown in blue) from corner to corner through the marked seam allowance (*not* the corners of the fabric rectangle). Place the rectangle right sides together with the print fabric, at the angle shown in the diagram, so the marked line touches the seam allowance below (**E2**). Put pins through these points if need be. Pin and then sew along the marked line (**E3**). Flip the triangle up and press (**E4**). When happy with the result, trim off excess Fabric 1 at the back – leave the print fabric uncut. Use this process when sewing any rectangle in place to create a triangle corner. On some pieces, the angle goes from top left to bottom right and may need to be across two fabric pieces, for example Unit 4 pieces **a**, **b** and **c**, as shown in **Fig F**. Sew pieces **a** and **b** together first.

6 Sewing Unit 2: Lay out the correct fabric pieces as shown in **Fig D**. Sew them together and press.

Fig E
Unit 1 – sewing piece **b** to **a**

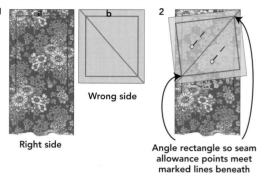

Mark the ¼in (6mm) seam allowances

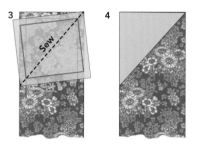

1 · a · b · Wrong side · Right side · **2** Angle rectangle so seam allowance points meet marked lines beneath · **3** Sew · **4**

Fig F
Unit 4 – sewing piece **c** to **a/b**

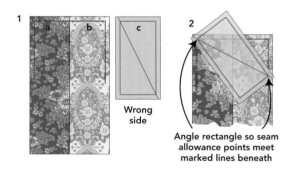

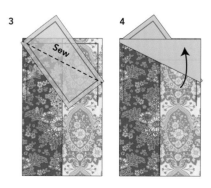

1 · a · b · c · Wrong side · **2** Angle rectangle so seam allowance points meet marked lines beneath · **3** Sew · **4**

7 Sewing Unit 3: Sew pieces **a** and **b** together and press. Add piece **c** to the top to create a rectangle triangle corner.

8 Sewing Unit 4: Sew pieces **a** and **b** together and press. Add piece **c** to the top to create a rectangle triangle corner (see **Fig F**). Now add piece **d** to the top of the unit.

9 Sewing Unit 5: Sew pieces **a** and **b** together and press. Add piece **c** to the bottom right to create a rectangle triangle corner. Add piece **d** to the top right to make another rectangle triangle corner. Note that these two triangles should overlap at the seam allowance on the right-hand edge. Add piece **e** to the top of the unit.

10 Sewing Unit 6: Place one triangle **b** and one triangle **c** right sides together, offsetting the pieces by ¼in (6mm) at the ends (don't match their end points). Sew together along the long, angled side. Press the seam open and trim to a unit 2½in x 1½in (6.4cm x 3.8cm).

Sew one triangle **d** and one triangle **e** together along the long, angled side. Press and trim to a unit 1½in (3.8cm) square. Sew **b/c** to **d/e** as shown in **Fig D**. Add piece **a** to the left-hand side and piece **f** to the right-hand side.

11 Sewing Unit 7: Sew one triangle **b** and one triangle **c** together along the long, angled side. Press and trim to a unit 2½in (6.4cm) square. Repeat to make another unit. Sew the units together as in **Fig D** and then add a piece **a** on the top and on the bottom.

Take a piece **d** and two **e** squares. Mark a diagonal line on the wrong side of the squares. Place them right side down on the print piece, with corner edges aligned and the marked line in the direction shown in **Fig G**. Sew on the marked line. Fold the triangle into place and press. Trim off excess Fabric 1 at the back. Repeat to make another unit. Now sew the two units together.

Sew one triangle **f** and one triangle **g** together along the long, angled side. Press and trim to 1½in (3.8cm) square. Repeat to make another unit but this time place the squares in the opposite corners. Follow the diagram to sew one **f/g** to the top of piece **h**, and the other **f/g** to the bottom.

Sew **a/b/c** to the left-hand side of **d/e**. Sew **f/g/h** to the right-hand side and press. Sew piece **i** to the top to complete Unit 7.

12 Now take all nine units and sew them together, following **Fig C** and pressing seams as you go. First, sew Units 1 to 5 together. Add Unit 6 to the bottom. Sew Unit 7 to the right-hand side. Add Unit 8 to the top.

13 Add Unit 9 on the left-hand side to complete the whale. The block should measure 40in x 10½in (101.6cm x 26.7cm). Make one more Whale block 1 like this.

MAKING WHALE BLOCKS 2, 3 AND 4

14 Make one Whale block 3 in the same way as block 1 but using the fabrics shown in **Fig H**.

15 Whale blocks 2 and 4 are made in the same way as block 1 but face the opposite way, so take great care when cutting the fabrics and piecing the units. Make two of Whale block 2 and one of Whale block 4.

Fig G
Unit 7 – sewing pieces **e** to **d**

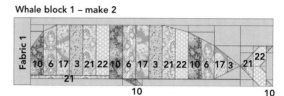

Fig H
Numbers indicate fabrics (which repeat across each whale)

Whale block 1 – make 2

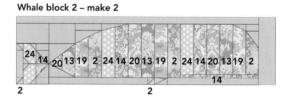

Whale block 2 – make 2

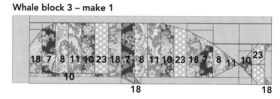

Whale block 3 – make 1

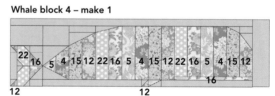

Whale block 4 – make 1

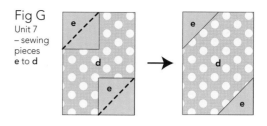

MAKING A PARTIAL WHALE BLOCK

16 The layout of a Partial Whale block is shown in **Fig I**. For one Partial Whale block 1 cut the following pieces.
a 2½in x 7½in (6.4cm x 19cm) in Fabric 10.
b 2½in x 2¾in (6.4cm x 7cm) in Fabric 1.
c 2½in x 1in (6.4cm x 2.5cm) in Fabric 1.
d 2½in x 8in (6.4cm x 20.3cm) in Fabric 6.
e 2½in x 1in (6.4cm x 2.5cm) in Fabric 1.
f 2½in x 8in (6.4cm x 20.3cm) in Fabric 17.
g 2½in x 8in (6.4cm x 20.3cm) in Fabric 3.
h 8½in x 1in (21.6cm x 2.5cm) in Fabric 21.
i 8½in x 1½in (21.6cm x 3.8cm) in Fabric 1.
j 8½in x 1½in (21.6cm x 3.8cm) in Fabric 1.
k 3in x 10½in (7.6cm x 26.7cm) in Fabric 1.

Fig I
Partial Whale block
Letters indicate fabric cut sizes

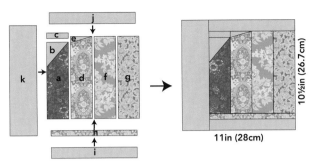

11in (28cm)

10½in (26.7cm)

Fig J
Numbers indicate fabrics

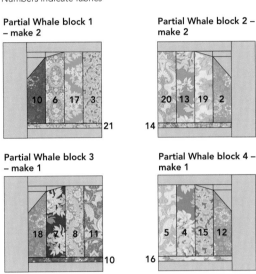

Partial Whale block 1 – make 2

10 6 17 3
21

Partial Whale block 2 – make 2

20 13 19 2
14

Partial Whale block 3 – make 1

18 7 8 11
10

Partial Whale block 4 – make 1

5 4 15 12
16

17 Sew the block together as shown in **Fig I**. Note that the assembly is essentially the same as Unit 1 for the full Whale block 1. The block should measure 11in x 10½in (28cm x 26.7cm). Make a total of two Partial Whale block 1.

18 For Partial Whale blocks 2, 3 and 4, repeat the cutting and assembly processes but using the fabrics shown in **Fig J**. Make two Partial Whale block 2 and one each of Partial Whale blocks 3 and 4. Note that blocks 2 and 4 face the opposite way to blocks 1 and 3.

ASSEMBLING THE QUILT
19 When all of the blocks and partial blocks have been made, lay them out in the order shown in **Fig B**. Sew the blocks together row by row. Now sew the rows together and press.

20 At the bottom of the quilt add a Fabric 1 strip 1½in x 50½in (3.8cm x 128.3cm). (You will need to join two pieces.) Press towards the thin strip.

QUILTING AND FINISHING
21 Prepare the backing fabric by cutting the fabric in half across the width. Sew the two pieces together down the long side and press the seam open. Trim to a piece about 58½in x 70in (149cm x 178cm). Make a quilt sandwich of the backing fabric, wadding (batting) and quilt. Quilt as desired. Square up the quilt, trimming excess wadding and backing.

22 Sew the buttons in place for the whale eyes (the positions are shown in **Fig B**). It is best to do this after all the quilting is finished, using a thread that tones with your backing fabric.

23 From Fabric 9 for the binding, cut six strips 2½in (6.4cm) x width of fabric. Sew together end to end and press seams open. Press in half along the length, wrong sides together. Use the prepared double-fold binding strip to bind your quilt (see General Techniques: Binding).

Whale Pillows

Perfect to accompany the Whale Quilt, these two pillows feature a blue whale and a pink whale block from the quilt. They use some of the same fabrics, so refer to the fabric swatches in **Fig A** of the quilt. The whale pillows are shown with some simple patchwork pillows. These are made using three of the blocks from the Beach Bags project.

MATERIALS

For one pillow

- Fabric 1: ⅜yd (40cm) – Solid warm sand
- Six print fabrics, ⅛yd (15cm) or about 10in (25.4cm) square of each
- Wadding (batting) 40in x 14in (101.5cm x 35.5cm)
- Lining fabric 40in x 14in (101.5cm x 35.5cm) (optional)
- Fabric for back of pillow, two pieces 22in x 11½in (56cm x 29.2cm)
- Binding fabric ¼yd (25cm)
- One ¾in (20mm) button for whale eye
- Three ¾in (20mm) buttons for pillow back (optional)
- Pillow pad about 37in x 11in (94cm x 28cm)

FINISHED SIZE

39in x 11in (99cm x 28cm)

MAKING A BLUE WHALE PILLOW

1 The blue whale pillow uses the same Whale block 3 as the Whale Quilt. The patchwork pieces for Units 1 to 8 are cut to the same sizes as the quilt, so use the sizes in step 3 of the quilt but using the fabrics in **Fig A** here. The border strips are slightly different to the quilt, so for one pillow also cut out the following pieces.

- Unit 9 – One 37½in x 1½in (95.3cm x 3.8cm) in Fabric 1.
- Unit 10 – One 1½in x 11½in (3.8cm x 29.2cm) in Fabric 1.
- Unit 11 – One 1½in x 11½in (3.8cm x 29.2cm) in Fabric 1.

You will find it easier to keep track of all of the pieces if you cut the pieces for one unit at a time and make the unit before moving on to the next one.

Fig A
Whale block 3
Numbers indicate fabrics – see Fig A of Whale Quilt project

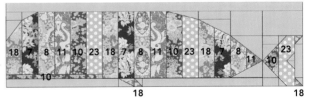

Fig B

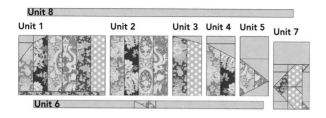

2 To piece the pillow, work on Unit 1, then Unit 2, Unit 3, and so on up to Unit 8. See **Fig B** for how these units go together and follow the instructions and diagrams carefully from the Whale Quilt, steps 4–12. Press seams open or to one side.

3 To finish the piecing, add the Unit 9 strip along the bottom of the block and the Unit 10 and Unit 11 strips to the sides of the block (**Fig C**) and press.

Fig C

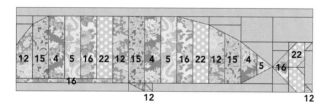

4 Make a quilt sandwich of the patchwork, wadding (batting) and lining fabric (if using). Quilt as desired. Sew the button in place for the eye.

5 The pillow is assembled with an overlapped back (with buttons to secure if you desire). Use the two pieces of back fabric and follow the instructions in General Techniques: Button-Fastening Cushion Cover.

6 The blue whale pillow uses Fabric 9 (Grandma's Rose blue) for the binding. Cut three 2½in (6.4cm) x width of fabric strips. Sew together and prepare as a double-fold binding. Now bind the cushion edge (see General Techniques: Binding).

Fig D
Whale block 4
Numbers indicate fabrics – see Fig A of Whale Quilt project

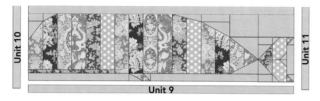

MAKING A PINK WHALE PILLOW

Sew the patchwork for this pillow in exactly the same way as the blue one but change the fabrics to those given in **Fig D** (see Whale Quilt, **Fig A** for the fabric swatches). Make up the pillow in the same way, using Fabric 19 (Grandma's Rose pink) for the binding.

Patchwork Octopus

This super-size octopus will always be fun to play with. The sixteen fabrics used are from the Sunkiss collection – simply pick your favourites.

MATERIALS

- Sixteen print fabrics for octopus: maximum of 21in x 7½in (53.5cm x 19cm) of each
- Thick paper for copying patterns
- Wooden stick or chopstick for turning and stuffing
- Toy stuffing (fibre fill)
- Dry rice, about eight tablespoons (about 160g/6oz)

FINISHED SIZE

9in x 25½in (23cm x 65cm)

MAKING THE OCTOPUS

1 Before you start, refer to General Techniques: Making Softies. Copy the patterns onto thick paper and cut out the shapes. Sixteen fabrics from the Sunkiss range were used for the head pieces. Some of the same fabrics were used randomly for the front and back of the legs. The eight fabrics used for the bottom of the octopus are the same as the back of the legs.

2 Cut a 3¾in x 21in (9.5cm x 53.5cm) piece from each of the fabrics. Pin two different fabric pieces right sides together. Draw the leg pattern on the fabric about ½in (1.3cm) away from the edge of the fabric and sew on the line leaving a gap where shown (**Fig A**). Cut out with a seam allowance, turn through and press. Fill the leg with a tablespoon of rice and then add the stuffing, *very loosely*. The rice will make the leg heavier and so hang better. Close the opening on top with a zigzag seam (**Fig B**). Repeat this with other pairs of fabrics, to make eight legs in total.

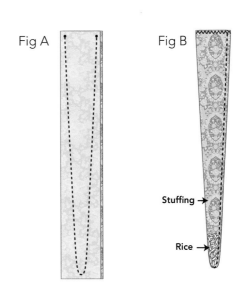

Fig A   Fig B

Stuffing →

Rice →

3 Using the remaining fabric, mark one head pattern on each of the sixteen fabrics and cut out the shapes with a ¼in (6mm) seam allowance all round. Match the head pieces up in pairs and then sew each pair together along one long side (**Fig C**), so that you have eight paired head pieces.

4 Using the triangle pattern and selecting the *same* fabrics as the back of the legs, mark eight bottom pieces. Cut out the shapes with a ¼in (6mm) seam allowance all round (**Fig D**).

5 Pin a head pair and bottom piece right sides together with a leg in between. The side of the leg that you want facing outwards on the finished octopus should face the head piece (see **Fig E**). Sew the pieces together along the bottom line. Fold the leg and bottom piece down (**Fig F**). Repeat this until you have eight pieces.

6 To assemble, start by placing two sections right sides together. Sew from the top of the head to the bottom of the bottom piece, keeping the legs out of the way (**Fig G**). Fold apart and sew the next section on. When sewing the last two edges together, all legs need to be *inside* the head (**Fig H**). Sew along the head and stop about ⅛in (3mm) into the bottom piece and secure the thread. Begin sewing again, this time about ⅛in (3mm) from the centre of the bottom and secure the thread, to leave a gap for turning through.

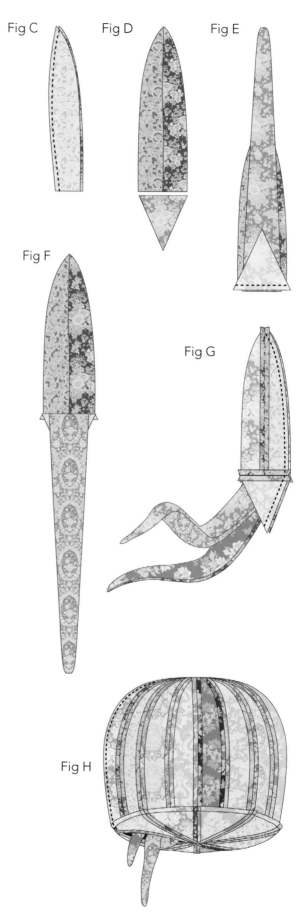

Fig C Fig D Fig E

Fig F

Fig G

Fig H

7 Bring all of the legs out through the opening and turn the head through. Stuff the head well and stitch the opening shut.

8 To cover the place where all the fabric ends meet on the top and bottom of the octopus, fold two pieces of fabric right sides together and draw two circles using the circle pattern. Sew all the way around (**Fig I**). Cut out the circles with a small seam allowance and make a slit through one of the fabric layers. Turn out through the slit and press. To finish, sew the circles onto the top and bottom of the octopus, with the slit facing in towards the octopus.

Fig I

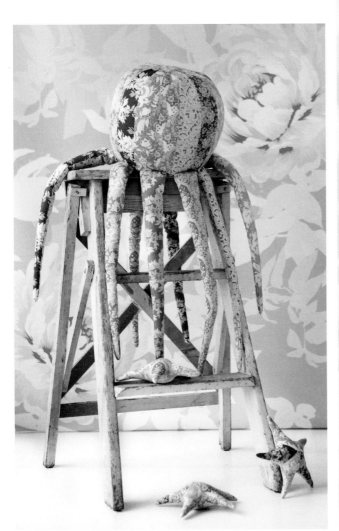

Starfish

This fun starfish makes a pretty decoration and continues the summer beach theme. You could also use it as a handy pincushion. It uses six fabrics from the Sunkiss collection.

MATERIALS

- Fabric 1 for starfish top: 3⅛in x 5⅛in (8cm x 13cm) – Suraj lilac
- Fabric 2 for starfish top: 3⅛in x 5⅛in (8cm x 13cm) – Charlotte teal
- Fabric 3 for starfish top: 3⅛in x 5⅛in (8cm x 13cm) – Imogen teal
- Fabric 4 for starfish top: 3⅛in x 5⅛in (8cm x 13cm) – Charlotte blue
- Fabric 5 for starfish top: 3⅛in x 5⅛in (8cm x 13cm) – Ocean Flower teal
- Fabric 6 for starfish bottom: 8⅝in x 8¼in (22cm x 21cm) – Imogen pink
- Wooden stick or chopstick for turning and stuffing
- Toy stuffing (fibre fill)
- Thick paper for copying patterns

FINISHED SIZE

7in x 7½in (18cm x 19cm)

MAKING THE STARFISH

1 Before you start, refer to the notes in General Techniques: Making Softies. Copy the patterns onto thick paper and cut out the shapes. The fabrics used are shown in **Fig A**.

Fig A

If you can't get hold of one or more of these fabrics, replace with fabric in similar colours

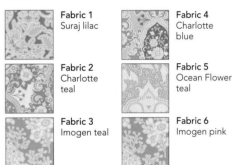

Fabric 1
Suraj lilac

Fabric 4
Charlotte blue

Fabric 2
Charlotte teal

Fabric 5
Ocean Flower teal

Fabric 3
Imogen teal

Fabric 6
Imogen pink

2 Start by cutting out the pieces. Place the starfish top pattern on the wrong side of Fabric 1 and draw the shape. Mark a ¼in (6mm) seam allowance all around the shape and then cut out the shape. Repeat this for Fabrics 2, 3, 4 and 5. Repeat the process again for the starfish bottom using Fabric 6.

Fig B

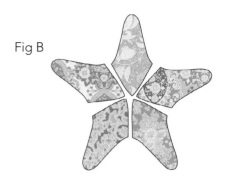

Fig C

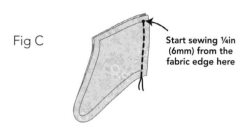

Start sewing ¼in (6mm) from the fabric edge here

Fig D

Gap

Fig E

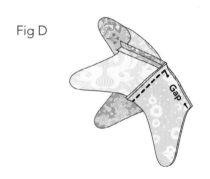

Fig F

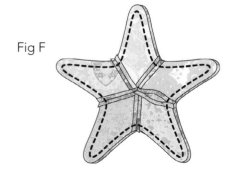

3 When the pieces are cut, place them in the order you like (**Fig B**). Place two of the shapes right sides together. Sew together along one short side, starting ¼in (6mm) away from the fabric edge that will be in the centre of the starfish, as shown in **Fig C**. Press the seam open. Repeat this to sew all five shapes together, aligning the seams neatly in the centre of the starfish (**Fig D**). When sewing the last seam leave a gap for turning through later (**Fig E**).

4 Place the top of the starfish right sides together with the bottom piece (re-draw the bottom pattern to match the top shape, if necessary). Pin together and then sew a ¼in (6mm) seam all around the edge (**Fig F**). Sew slowly around the tight curves, pivoting the needle as needed to achieve smooth curves. Trim the seam allowance if necessary. Snip notches in the tight inward curves between each leg.

5 Turn through to the right side, using a wooden stick to help turn out the points. Fill the starfish with stuffing, using the wooden stick to ensure the points are well stuffed. Sew up the gap with tiny slipstitches and matching thread.

Mermaids

Adorable mermaids like these are sure to become favourite softie toys. Three different mermaids are shown, with instructions for the teal-tailed one.

MATERIALS

- Fabric 1: one fat quarter – Suraj lilac
- Fabric 2: one fat quarter – Charlotte teal
- Fabric 3: 6in (15.2cm) square – Ocean Flower teal
- Fabric 4: one fat quarter – Doll fabric
- Fusible web 10in (25.5cm) square
- Toy stuffing (fibre fill)
- Black hobby paint and a big ball-headed pin or thin brush for eyes
- Lipstick or rouge and a dry brush for rosy cheeks
- Thick paper for copying patterns

FINISHED SIZE

12½in (32cm) tall

MAKING THE MERMAID

1 Before you start, refer to the notes in General Techniques: Making Softies. Copy all the pattern pieces onto thick paper and cut out the shapes. Four fabrics are used for the patchwork (see **Fig A**).

Fig A

If you can't get hold of one or more of these fabrics, replace with fabric in similar colours

Fabric 1
Suraj lilac

Fabric 3
Ocean Flower teal

Fabric 2
Charlotte teal

Fabric 4
Doll fabric

Fig B

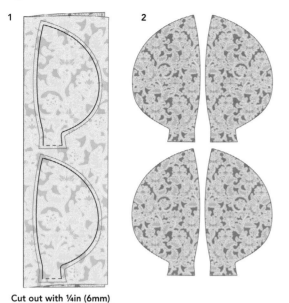

Cut out with ¼in (6mm)
seam allowance all round

Fig C

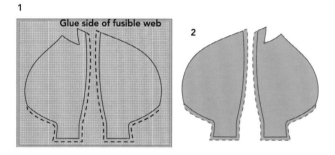

Glue side of fusible web

Fig D

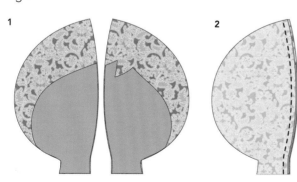

2 Head: For the head, cut a 10¼in (26cm) wide x 15¾in (40cm) high piece of Fabric 1. Fold it in half, right sides together, and draw two head shapes as in **Fig B1**. Cut out the shapes with an added ¼in (6mm) seam allowance all round. You will then have four head shapes, as in **Fig B2**. Cut another piece from Fabric 1, 8½in (21.6cm) wide x 2¾in (7cm) high, to prepare the hair bun shapes later.

3 For the face, cut a piece of Fabric 4 (doll fabric) 8in (20.3cm) wide x 6½in (16.5cm) high. Cut a piece of fusible web the same size and iron it onto the back of the fabric. Once cool, remove the paper, leaving only the glue web. Place the face patterns *face down* on the glue side of the fabric and draw the shapes, including the seam allowance on the areas marked with dashed lines (**Fig C**). Cut out the shapes with sharp scissors, including the marked seam allowance, and cutting on the line along the hairline.

4 Iron the face shapes glue side down against the right side of two of the head shapes (**Fig D1**). Place these two shapes right sides together and sew as in **Fig D2**. Sew the two pieces for the back of the head together in the same way. Press the seams open.

Fig E

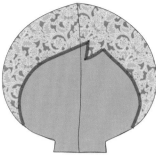

Fig F

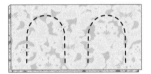

Fig G

5 With the face flat, right side up, sew along the hairline with a very dense machine zigzag stitch using a skin-coloured thread (**Fig E**). Place the two head pieces right sides together and sew around the edge (**Fig F**). On the neck opening, fold in the extra seam allowance before pressing. Stuff the head well to get a good shape, leaving the neck open.

6 For the hair buns, take the piece of Fabric 1 you cut earlier. Fold it in half, right sides together and use the pattern to draw two hair buns. Sew the shapes as shown in **Fig G**. Cut the pieces out with a small seam allowance all round. Turn right side out and fold in the extra seam allowance before pressing. Stuff each bun.

Fig H

1

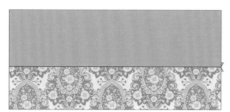

2

Fig I

Fig J

Fig K

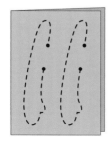

7 Body: For the body, cut a piece of Fabric 4 about 14in x 4½in (35.6cm x 11.4cm) and a piece of Fabric 2 about 14in x 3½in (35.6cm x 9cm). Use a ¼in (6mm) seam to sew the pieces together and press the seam open (**Fig H1**). Fold the pieced fabric in half, right sides together. Place the body pattern on the fabric, with the dashed line of the pattern horizontally on the seamline. Mark the pattern and then sew along the marked line (**H2**). Cut out with a seam allowance all round. Turn through to the right side and fold in the extra seam allowance before pressing. Stuff the body, leaving the bottom open.

8 Tail: For the tail, take the remaining piece of Fabric 2, a piece about 14in x 5½in (35.6cm x 14cm), and fold it in half, right sides together. Mark and then sew the tail pattern (**Fig I**). Cut out with a seam allowance, turn through, press and stuff. Insert the extra seam allowance of the tail into the opening in the body. Sew the opening shut (**Fig J**).

9 Arms: For the arms, from Fabric 4 cut a piece 6¼in (16cm) square. Fold it in half, right sides together. Mark the arm pattern twice and sew on the line, leaving an opening in the seam for turning, as marked on the pattern (**Fig K**). Cut out with a seam allowance and use a wooden stick to turn through. Press and then stuff.

10 Starfish: For the starfish, take the piece of Fabric 3 and fold in half, right sides together. Mark the star pattern twice and sew on the line around the shapes (**Fig L**). Cut out with a small seam allowance and snip into the inward curves. On each star, cut a slit through one layer of fabric. Turn through to the right side, press and stuff lightly, using a wooden stick. Sew the stars to the mermaid's upper body, with the slits face down.

Fig L

Fig M

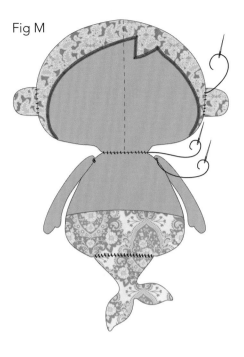

Fig N

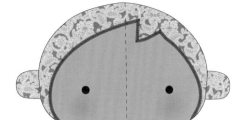

ASSEMBLING AND FINISHING

11 Tack (baste) the head onto the top of the body, so the neck opening is open against the curve of the body, and then sew securely in place (**Fig M**). Hand sew the stuffed hair buns in place on each side of the head. Sew the arms to the body.

12 To make the face, use black hobby paint for the eyes and lipstick or rouge for the cheeks. Use a big ball-headed pin to mark where the eyes will be and wiggle the pin to make a hole. Dip the head of the pin in paint and stamp eyes (**Fig N**). If you don't have this kind of pin, find something else to use as a stamp, or draw circles about ¼in (6mm) in diameter, and paint on eyes with a thin brush. Once the eyes are dry, mark rosy cheeks with lipstick or rouge and a dry brush.

Beach Bags

These cheerful beach bags are perfect for summer days at the beach, or if you need a roomy bag for shopping. Patchwork panels are used for the front and back of the bag and shoulder straps make carrying easy. The bags use fabrics from the Sunkiss collection. The blue version is described in detail.

MATERIALS

For the blue bag

- Fabric 1: ¼yd (25cm) or fat quarter – Charlotte ginger
- Fabric 2: ⅜yd (40cm) or fat quarter – Beach Peony blue
- Fabric 3: ¼yd (25cm) or fat quarter – Grandma's Rose blue
- Fabric 4: ⅜yd (40cm) or fat quarter – Suraj lilac
- Fabric 5: ¼yd (25cm) or fat quarter – Beach Peony ginger
- Fabric 6: ¼yd (25cm) or fat quarter – Ocean Flower blue
- Fabric 7: ¼yd (25cm) or fat quarter – Imogen blue
- Fabric 8: Grandma's Rose lilac (included in lining fabric amount, below)
- Fabric 9: ⅛yd (15cm) – Ocean Flower teal
- Fabric 10: ⅛yd (15cm) – Imogen teal
- Fabric 11: ⅛yd (15cm) – Imogen pink
- Bag lining fabric 1½yd (1.3m) – Grandma's Rose lilac
- Backing fabric (such as calico) 29in x 51in (73.7cm x 129.5cm)
- Wadding (batting): one piece 29in x 51in (73.7cm x 129.5cm) and two pieces 3in x 26½in (7.6cm x 67.3cm)

FINISHED SIZE

28in x 24½in (71cm x 62.2cm) approx., excluding handles

Fig A

Fabric swatches for both bags

If you can't get hold of one or more of these fabrics, replace with fabric in similar colours

Fabric 1
Charlotte ginger

Fabric 2
Beach Peony blue

Fabric 3
Grandma's Rose blue

Fabric 4
Suraj lilac

Fabric 5
Beach Peony ginger

Fabric 6
Ocean Flower blue

Fabric 7
Imogen blue

Fabric 8
Grandma's Rose lilac

Fabric 9
Ocean Flower teal

Fabric 10
Imogen teal

Fabric 11
Imogen pink

Fabric 12
Charlotte teal

Fabric 13
Beach Peony teal

Fabric 14
Ocean Flower pink

Fabric 15
Beach Peony lime

Fabric 16
Charlotte pink

Fabric 17
Suraj teal

Fabric 18
Grandma's Rose pink

MAKING THE BLUE BAG

1 These instructions describe the blue version of the bag, which uses Fabrics 1 to 11 (see swatches in **Fig A**). The lime/teal version of the bag uses Fabrics 9 to 19. The bag has a patchwork panel made up of six blocks for the bag front, with a second identical panel for the bag back. There are six blocks in a panel and each block is made up of four sizes – A, B, C and D. **Fig B** shows the cut sizes for the pieces. Follow **Fig C** carefully to cut the pieces. The letters on the diagram indicate the cut sizes and the numbers indicate the fabrics used. Cut two pieces 29in x 25½in (73.7cm x 64.8cm) from Fabric 8 (the lining fabric) *before* you cut the smaller pieces for the patchwork.

- A = 4in x 5½in (10.2cm x 14cm).
- B = 6½in x 9½in (16.5cm x 24.1cm).
- C = 4in x 8in (10.2cm x 20.3cm).
- D = 6½in x 4in (16.5cm x 10.2cm).

2 Lay out the cut fabric pieces in six blocks as in **Fig C**. Taking one block at a time, sew the pieces together in two columns and then join to finish the block. Repeat with all six blocks. Each block should be 10in x 13in (25.5cm x 33cm). Now join the six blocks together in rows and then sew the rows together. Press the panel. Repeat this process to make an identical panel for the back of the bag. Each panel should be 29in x 25½in (73.7cm x 64.8cm). Sew the two panels together as in **Fig D** and press.

3 To make the lining bag, take the two pieces of lining cut earlier. Sew together, leaving an opening in the seam for turning through later.

4 To make a handle cut a 7in x 4in (17.8cm x 10.2cm) rectangle from Fabrics 9, 1, 7 and 8. Sew them together in this order and press seams open. Repeat with the same size pieces of Fabrics 4, 2, 3 and 5. Each handle will be 26½in (67.3cm) long. Cut two strips of wadding (batting) the same length but 3in (7.6cm) wide. Place a wadding strip against the back of each handle patchwork. Fold in and press the fabric edges (**Fig E**). Fold each strip double so that each handle is about 1½in (3.8cm) wide. Topstitch along both sides.

Fig B
Cut sizes of fabric pieces

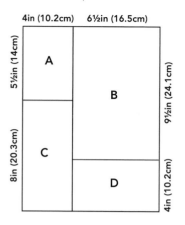

Fig C

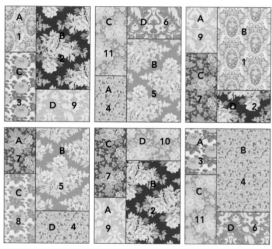

Fig D

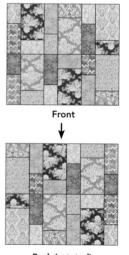

Front ↓

Back (rotated)

Fig E

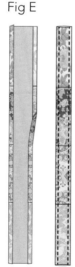

Fig F

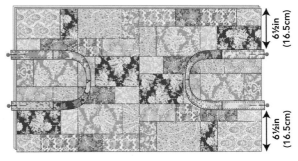

6½in (16.5cm)

6½in (16.5cm)

Fig G

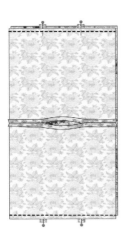

Fig H

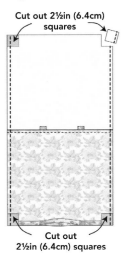

Cut out 2½in (6.4cm) squares

Cut out 2½in (6.4cm) squares

Fig I

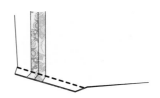

8 Turn the bag right side out through the opening in the lining and press. Push the lining into the bag. Topstitch along the top of the bag, about ½in (1.3cm) in from the edge to keep the lining in place. Sew the opening in the lining closed to finish.

MAKING THE LIME BAG

The lime/teal version of the bag uses Fabrics 9 to 18 (see swatches in **Fig A**). Make it in exactly the same way as the blue bag. Fabric 16 (Charlotte pink) is used for the lining.

5 Layer the bag patchwork with the same size of wadding (batting) and backing fabric. Quilt as desired.

6 Pin the handles on the right side of the quilted patchwork piece, about 6½in (16.5cm) from each corner. The handles must point in towards the patchwork, as in **Fig F**.

7 Place the lining right side down on top of the patchwork and sew a seam along the top and bottom edge (**Fig G**). Fold the bag so that the two patchwork halves lie right side against each other, and the two lining halves lie against each other on the opposite side. The seams where the handles are attached should be in the middle. Sew the pieces together along the edge on the right and the left side (**Fig H**). To create depth to the bag, cut out a 2½in (6.4cm) square in each of the four corners, as shown. Fold each corner so that the seam is in the middle and then sew across as in **Fig I**.

Sailing Regatta Quilt

Serene sail boats float past on this lovely quilt. The boats are created with many different blocks, so you will need to follow the instructions and diagrams carefully, but the finished effect will be well worth the effort. The quilt uses fabrics from the Lemontree and Sunkiss ranges, plus three solid fabrics.

MATERIALS

- Fabric 1: 1¼yd (1.2m) – Solid dove white
- Fabric 2: 1¼yd (1.2m) – Solid warm sand
- Fabric 3: 4yd (3.7m) – Solid soft teal
- Fabric 4: ¼yd (25cm) – Imogen pink
- Fabric 5: ¼yd (25cm) – Imogen teal
- Fabric 6: ⅛yd (15cm) – Imogen blue
- Fabric 7: ¼yd (25cm) – Suraj teal
- Fabric 8: ¼yd (25cm) – Imogen green
- Fabric 9: ⅛yd (15cm) – Flowerfield red
- Fabric 10: ⅛yd (15cm) – Lemontree yellow
- Fabric 11: ¼yd (25cm) – Boogie Flower red
- Fabric 12: ⅛yd (15cm) – Mosaics red
- Fabric 13: ⅛yd (15cm) – Flowerfield blue
- Fabric 14: ⅛yd (15cm) – Lemonade ginger
- Fabric 15: ⅛yd (15cm) – Lemontree plum
- Backing fabric 5yd (4.6m) – Lemontree yellow
- Wadding (batting) 63in x 90in (160cm x 229cm)
- Binding fabric ½yd (50cm) – Lemontree yellow

FINISHED SIZE

54in x 81in (137cm x 206cm)

Fig A

If you can't get hold of one or more of these fabrics, replace with fabric in similar colours

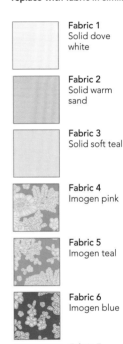

Fabric 1
Solid dove white

Fabric 2
Solid warm sand

Fabric 3
Solid soft teal

Fabric 4
Imogen pink

Fabric 5
Imogen teal

Fabric 6
Imogen blue

Fabric 7
Suraj teal

Fabric 8
Imogen green

Fabric 9
Flowerfield red

Fabric 10
Lemontree yellow

Fabric 11
Boogie Flower red

Fabric 12
Mosaics red

Fabric 13
Flowerfield blue

Fabric 14
Lemonade ginger

Fabric 15
Lemontree plum

1 Before you start, refer to General Techniques: Making Quilts and Pillows. Twelve print fabrics are used in the quilt, plus three solid fabrics (see **Fig A**). The quilt is made up of six mega-blocks – all made the same way. In each mega-block there are twenty-two different blocks (Blocks A to V). Six of these are repeated in different colourways. See **Fig B** for the quilt layout.

2 The number of different blocks may seem daunting, but only a few techniques are needed and these are repeated in many of the blocks. **Fig C** shows all of the blocks, with the fabrics used and the numbers of each block to make. Detailed instructions follow for each block.

Fig B
Quilt layout

Fig C
The various blocks used in the quilt
Numbers within the blocks indicate the fabrics used

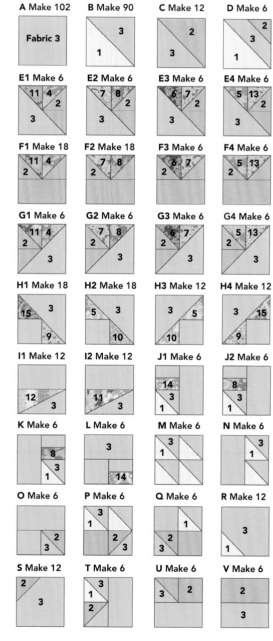

60

Fig D
Total numbers of cut pieces needed for the quilt

3½in x 3½in (9cm x 9cm)

Fabric 1 Cut 96 | Fabric 2 Cut 12 | Fabric 3 Cut 342

3½in x 2in (9cm x 5cm)

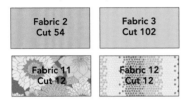

Fabric 2 Cut 54 | Fabric 3 Cut 102
Fabric 11 Cut 12 | Fabric 12 Cut 12

2in x 2in (5cm x 5cm)

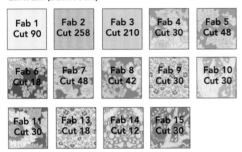

Fab 1 Cut 90 | Fab 2 Cut 258 | Fab 3 Cut 210 | Fab 4 Cut 30 | Fab 5 Cut 48
Fab 6 Cut 18 | Fab 7 Cut 48 | Fab 8 Cut 42 | Fab 9 Cut 30 | Fab 10 Cut 30
Fab 11 Cut 30 | Fab 13 Cut 18 | Fab 14 Cut 12 | Fab 15 Cut 30

Fig E
Making a half-square triangle unit

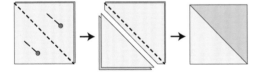

3 You may want to cut all the pieces for the blocks at the start, or cut them as you go along. **Fig D** shows the total numbers of cut pieces needed for the whole quilt. Sizes include ¼in (6mm) seam allowances.

MAKING HALF-SQUARE TRIANGLE UNITS

4 Many of the blocks need half-square triangle (HST) units. For this quilt these have been made using two squares to create a single HST unit (there is some fabric wastage with this method). Two different sizes are needed – large and small – so use the following square sizes.

- Large HST – use a 3½in (9cm) square of two different fabrics. When sewn, this will make a 3½in (9cm) square unit (unfinished). (See also Tip, below.)

- Small HST – use a 2in (5cm) square of two different fabrics. When sewn, this will make a 2in (5cm) square unit (unfinished).

Follow the process shown in **Fig E**. Start by marking a diagonal line on the wrong side (WS) of one of the squares. Place the squares right sides (RS) together and sew along the marked line. Trim excess fabric ¼in (6mm) away from the sewn line and then press the HST unit open.

> **Tip** When making the large 3½in (9cm) half-square triangles, sew an extra seam line ½in (1.3cm) away from the centre seam. Cut the units apart and you will have a 'free', smaller HST unit (**Fig F**). You can use these for other projects or trim them down to 2in (5cm) square and use them for this quilt.

Fig F
Creating a 'free' HST

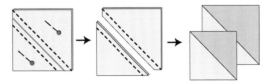

MAKING THE BLOCKS

5 The following steps describe the cutting out and making of the blocks. Follow **Fig C** carefully for the fabrics used and the total numbers of blocks to make. Once sewn, check each block is 3½in (9cm) square. Label the blocks as you make them, so you can identify them easily later. Label your spare HST units too, so you can use them when making repeat blocks.

Block A: This is just a 3½in (9cm) square of Fabric 3.

Block B: Make a large HST using Fabrics 1 and 3 (see step 4).

Block C: Make a large HST using Fabrics 2 and 3.

6 Block D: Make a large HST using Fabrics 1 and 3. Place a 2in (5cm) square of Fabric 2 in the top right corner, right sides together (**Fig G**). Sew along the diagonal, trim off excess fabric and press the corner triangle into place.

7 Block E: Block E 1 is described here. Make one small HST (see step 4) using Fabrics 2 and 4. Sew the HST together with a 2in (5cm) square of Fabric 11 and Fabric 2, as in **Fig H**. On a 3½in (9cm) square of Fabric 3 mark the diagonal line. Place the square right sides together with the units, aligning the straight edges. Sew along the marked line. Trim off excess fabric ¼in (6mm) away from the sewn line and then open out the triangle and press the block. Make Blocks E 2, E 3 and E 4 the same way but change fabrics as in **Fig C**.

8 Block F: Block F 1 is described here. Make one small HST using Fabrics 2 and 11 and another small HST using Fabrics 2 and 4. Sew the HSTs together as in **Fig I**. Add a 2in x 3½in (5cm x 9cm) rectangle of Fabric 2 to the bottom. Make Blocks F 2, F 3 and F 4 the same way but change fabrics as in **Fig C**.

9 Block G: Make Blocks G 1, G 2, G 3 and G 4 in the same way as Block E, using the fabrics in **Fig C**. Note that the layout of the block is reflected (flipped).

10 Block H: Make Blocks H 1, H 2, H 3 and H 4 in the same way as Block E but using a 2in (5cm) square instead of a small HST unit. Follow the fabrics and layouts shown in **Fig C**.

Fig G
Making Block D

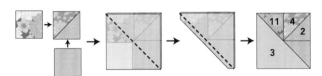

Fig H
Making Block E

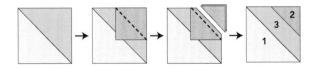

Fig I
Making Block F

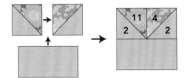

Fig J

Making Block I

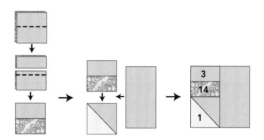

Fig K

Making Block J

11 Block I: Block I 1 is described here. To make the half-rectangle triangle take a 2in x 3½in (5cm x 9cm) rectangle of Fabric 3 and Fabric 12. Mark the diagonal line on the wrong side of one of the rectangles. Place it right sides together with the second rectangle, at the angle shown in **Fig J**. Sew along the marked line. Trim excess fabric ¼in (6mm) away from the sewn line. Fold the triangle into place and press. Sew a rectangle of Fabric 3 to the top. Make Block I 2 in the same way but using Fabrics 3 and 11.

12 Block J: Block J 1 is described here. To make a two-rectangles unit, take a 2in (5cm) square of Fabric 3 and Fabric 14. Put them right sides together and mark a line across the exact centre. Sew on the marked line. Trim a ¼in (6mm) away from the line and press the unit open (**Fig K**). Make a small HST from Fabrics 1 and 3. Sew the two units together. Sew a 2in x 3½in (5cm x 9cm) rectangle of Fabric 3 to the right-hand side of the block. Make Block J 2 in the same way but using Fabrics 1, 3 and 8.

13 Block K: Make Block K in the same way as Block J but with the rectangle on the left-hand side and using the fabrics in **Fig C**.

14 Block L: Make a two-rectangles unit as you did in Block J using 2in (5cm) squares of Fabrics 3 and 14. Sew a 2in (5cm) square of Fabric 3 to the left side. Sew a 2in x 3½in (5cm x 9cm) rectangle of Fabric 3 to the top.

15 Block M: Make four small HSTs from Fabrics 1 and 3. Sew them together as in **Fig C**.

16 Block N: Make two small HSTs from Fabrics 1 and 3. Sew them together with a 2in x 3½in (5cm x 9cm) rectangle of Fabric 3.

17 Block O: Make a small HST from Fabrics 2 and 3. Sew it together with a 2in (5cm) square and a 2in x 3½in (5cm x 9cm) rectangle of Fabric 3, as in **Fig C**.

18 Block P: Make three small HSTs – two from Fabrics 1 and 3 and one from Fabrics 2 and 3. Sew the HSTs together with a 2in (5cm) square of Fabric 2, as in **Fig C**.

19 Block Q: Make two small HSTs – one from Fabrics 1 and 3 and one from Fabrics 2 and 3. Sew the HSTs together with a 2in (5cm) square of Fabric 2 and one of Fabric 3, as in **Fig C**.

20 Block R: Take a 3½in (9cm) square of Fabric 3 and a 2in (5cm) square of Fabric 1. Sew the small square to the large one, as you did for Block D. Trim off excess fabric and press the corner triangle outwards.

21 Block S: Make the same way as Block R and using the fabrics in **Fig C**.

22 Block T: Make two small HSTs – one from Fabrics 1 and 3 and one from Fabrics 2 and 3. Sew together and add a 2in x 3½in (5cm x 9cm) rectangle of Fabric 3 to the right-hand side.

23 Block U: Make the same way as Block O but with the rectangle on the bottom, and using the fabrics in **Fig C**.

24 Block V: Sew together two rectangles 3½in x 2in (9cm x 5cm) of Fabric 2 and Fabric 3.

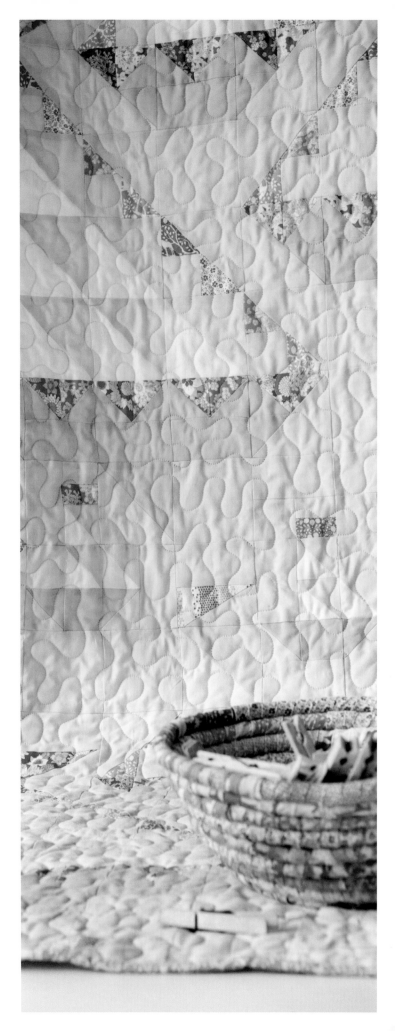

Fig L
Assembling a mega-block

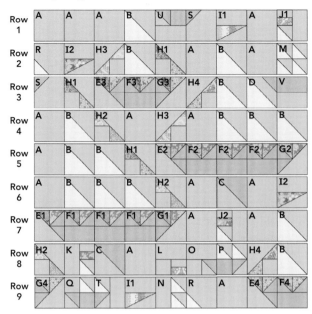

Row 1	A	A	A	B	U	S	I1	A	J1
Row 2	R	I2	H3	B	H1	A	B	A	M
Row 3	S	H1	E3	F3	G3	H4	B	D	V
Row 4	A	B	H2	A	H3	A	B	B	B
Row 5	A	B	B	H1	E2	F2	F2	F2	G2
Row 6	A	B	B	B	H2	A	C	A	I2
Row 7	E1	F1	F1	F1	G1	A	J2	A	B
Row 8	H2	K	C	A	L	O	P	H4	B
Row 9	G4	Q	T	I1	N	R	A	E4	F4

ASSEMBLING THE QUILT

25 Check that all of the blocks are 3½in (9cm) square. Follow **Fig L** very carefully to lay out the first mega-block, which has nine rows each with nine blocks. Sew the blocks together in rows, pressing the seams of Rows 1, 3, 5, 7 and 9 in one direction and Rows 2, 4, 6 and 8 in the opposite direction. Now sew the rows together, matching seams neatly, and press. Repeat to assemble five more mega-blocks.

26 Lay out the six mega-blocks as in **Fig B**. Sew them together and press.

QUILTING AND FINISHING

27 Cut the backing fabric into two pieces across the width. Sew together along the long sides and press the seam open. Trim to a piece about 63in x 90in (160cm x 229cm). Make a quilt sandwich of the backing fabric, wadding (batting) and quilt. Quilt as desired. Square up the quilt, trimming excess wadding and backing.

28 From the binding fabric cut seven 2½in (6.4cm) x width of fabric strips. Sew them together end to end and press seams open. Fold in half along the length wrong sides together. Use the prepared double-fold binding strip to bind your quilt (see General Techniques: Binding).

Materials

Tilda fabrics and other materials are used predominantly for the projects in this book. The print fabrics come from the Lemontree and Sunkiss collections. If you are unable to get hold of a fabric you can easily replace it with another fabric of similar colour, including fabrics from other Tilda collections. Many of the smaller projects only use small quantities of fabrics and you can put your off-cuts to good use. Plain-dyed and solid dove white fabric is used in most of the patchwork projects as a contrast to the print fabrics. Tilda doll fabric is used for the Mermaid's skin. See the Tilda fabric collections and related products at: www.tildasworld.com.

QUILT BACKING FABRIC

The quilt instructions give the yardage needed for backing fabric. These amounts allow 4in (10.2cm) extra all round, to allow the quilt to be long-arm quilted. If quilting the project yourself then 2in (5cm) extra all round will be sufficient. The yardage given is based on the normal 42in–44in (107cm–112cm) wide fabric. If you use a wider fabric then the amount needed will need to be re-calculated. You can also sew quilting fabrics together to make a piece big enough for a backing.

WADDING (BATTING)

The wadding used is your choice and depends on the effect you want to achieve. For a normal flat and firm result, cotton wadding is recommended, especially for the quilts and pillows. If you like a puffy look then a wadding with a higher loft can be used. Cut the wadding the same size as the backing.

GENERAL MATERIALS AND TOOLS

The project instructions give the fabrics that are needed but you will also need some general materials and tools, including the following.

- Piecing and quilting threads.

- Rotary cutter and mat.

- Quilter's ruler – a 6½in x 24in (16.5cm x 61cm) rectangular ruler and a 12in (30.5cm) square ruler are most useful.

- Sharp fabric scissors.

- Hand sewing and embroidery needles, and pins.

- Marking tools, such as a water-soluble pen or chalk liner.

- Thick paper or template plastic to make templates.

General Techniques

This section describes the general techniques you will need for the project. Techniques that are specific to a project are given within the project instructions.

USING THE PATTERNS

All of the patterns for the book are given full size in the Patterns section at the end of the book. To prepare a pattern, trace or photocopy it onto thick paper (including all marks) and cut out the shape. Label the pattern. If a pattern is made up of two or more parts, then use adhesive tape to fix them together along the dashed lines. There are notes at the start of the Patterns section giving further guidance.

MAKING SOFTIES

Follow these general guidelines when making the soft projects in the book.

• Read a project's instructions before you start.

• The paper patterns for each softie are in the Patterns section, so follow instructions there.

• A piece of fabric may be used for several pattern pieces, so position and cut pieces economically.

• Use a shorter stitch length of about 1.5mm for seams that will be stuffed later.

• Where a gap needs to be left, backstitch at both ends to secure the sewing line.

• To get a good shape, cut snips in the seam allowance where seams curve tightly inwards.

• Stuff well, using a wooden stick to make sure you fill small areas such as arms and ears.

• Sew up gaps with matching thread and small slipstitches.

FACES

To make eyes, we suggest using black hobby paint. Mark their positions first with a pin. For big eyes ¼in (6mm) diameter, as used in the cat, use a large ball-headed pin. To mark where the eyes will be, wiggle the pin until you have a visible hole. Dip the head of the pin in paint and then stamp eyes on the project. You could also find something else to use as a stamp, or draw circles and paint on eyes with a thin brush.

SAFETY

When you sew a toy yourself do ensure that it is safe. Bear in mind the following points, especially when sewing for children.

• Don't let children use toys if small parts or buttons have been used in them.

• Be aware that children can be allergic to some materials, so choose with care.

• Make toys strong and resistant to wear and tear by double sewing seams and fastening legs and arms and other loose parts in place securely with strong embroidery thread.

• Take great care not to leave pins or needles in toys.

WASHING

Stuffed toys are not suitable for washing as the stuffing can move about or become uneven. To clean a toy, wipe it with a damp cloth. If Tilda rouge has been used, this is water-soluble and can be re-applied. Quilts and pillow covers can be machine washed at 40-degrees.

QUILTING

There are many ways to quilt a project. For the quilts in this book you could machine or hand stitch 'in the ditch' (in the seams) of each block. Another method is to quilt about ¼in (6mm) away from the seams.

BINDING

The binding used for the projects in the book is a double-fold binding, using strips cut 2½in (6.4cm) wide x width of fabric. You can sew the binding strips together using straight seams, or diagonal (45-degree) seams if you prefer.

1 Press the binding in half all along the length, wrong sides together.

2 Follow **Fig A**. Sew the binding to the quilt by pinning the raw edge of the binding against the raw edge of the quilt front. Don't start at a corner. Using a ¼in (6mm) seam, sew the binding in place, starting at least 6in (15.2cm) away from the end of the binding. Sew to within a ¼in (6mm) of a corner and stop. Take the quilt off the machine and fold the binding upwards, creating a 45-degree angle. Fold the binding back down and pin it in place. Begin sewing the ¼in (6mm) seam again from the top of the folded binding to within ¼in (6mm) of the next corner and then repeat the folding process. Do this on all corners. Leave about 6in (15.2cm) of unsewn binding at the end.

MAKING QUILTS AND PILLOWS

Follow these general guidelines when making the quilts and pillows in the book.

- Read all the instructions through before you start.
- Fabric quantities are based on a usable width of 42in (107cm).
- Measurements are in imperial inches with metric conversions in brackets – use only *one* system throughout (preferably imperial as the projects were made using this system).
- Press fabrics before cutting.
- Use ¼in (6mm) seams unless otherwise instructed.
- Press seams open or to one side, as preferred, or according to the project instructions.

QUILT SANDWICH

If you are quilting the quilt yourself you will need to make a quilt sandwich. Press the quilt top and the backing and smooth wrinkles out of the wadding (batting). Place the backing fabric right side down, place the wadding on top and then the quilt, right side up. Secure the layers of this sandwich with pins, tacking (basting) or spray glue and then quilt as desired.

Fig A

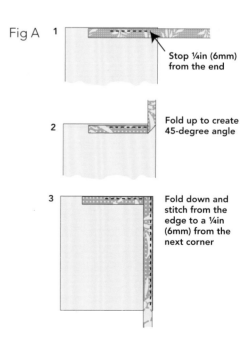

1 Stop ¼in (6mm) from the end

2 Fold up to create 45-degree angle

3 Fold down and stitch from the edge to a ¼in (6mm) from the next corner

3 To join the two ends of the binding, open up the beginning and end of the binding tails, lay them flat and fold the ends back so the two ends touch. Mark these folds by creasing or with pins. Open out the binding and sew the pieces together at these creases with a straight seam. Trim off excess fabric and press the seam. Re-fold the binding and finish stitching it in place on the front of the quilt.

4 With the quilt right side up, press the binding outwards all round. Now begin to turn the binding over to the back of the quilt, pinning it in place. Use matching sewing thread and tiny stitches to slipstitch the binding in place all round, creating neat mitres at each corner. Press to finish.

CUSHION COVER

The most popular cushion cover doesn't usually have any fastenings but just a hemmed opening on the back of the cover, which overlaps at the centre (**Fig B**).

1 Start by calculating the size of the two backing pieces needed, as follows. Measure the width of the cushion or pillow, divide this number in half and then add 4in (10cm). So, for a 20in (50cm) wide pillow, this would be 20in ÷ 2 = 10in (25cm) + 4in (10cm) = 14in (35cm). The height of the pieces will be the same as the front of the cushion. On both pieces of fabric along the short sides, make a hem by turning the edge over by ½in (1.3cm), twice. Sew with matching thread and press.

2 Place the patchwork front right side up. Pin one backing piece on top, right side down, hem towards the centre. Pin the second backing piece on top, right side down, hem towards the centre. Make sure the outer edges of all three pieces are aligned.

3 To assemble the cover *without* a binding, sew the layers together around the outside, using a ¼in–⅜in (6mm–10mm) seam. Remove pins and press. Turn through to the right side and press.

4 To assemble the cover *with* a binding, pin or tack (baste) the layers together but this time with right sides facing *out*, and then bind as normal. As you sew the binding in place it will fix the other layers together.

Fig B   1   2

Button-Fastening Cushion Cover

You can add buttons to the back of your cushion covers if you want, as a decoration and a fastening. Make the cushion cover as described above but allow for a wider hem on the backing pieces where they meet in the centre. Use your sewing machine to make buttonholes along one hem. Sew the buttons on the other hem, to correspond with the buttonholes.

Patterns

- You can download printable versions of the patterns from: http://ideas.sewandso.co.uk/patterns.

- All of the patterns are given full size.

- The patterns are shown in different colours to distinguish them from other patterns.

- The outer solid line on a pattern is the sewing line, unless otherwise stated.

- Dashed lines on pattern edges show openings.

- Dashed blue lines show where two parts of a pattern have to be joined (e.g. by A and B points, which need to be matched).

- Dashed lines inside patterns show a division between two fabrics. For the Lemonade Quilt patterns, dashed lines show the seam allowance.

- Short lines on the edges of a pattern show where fabric pieces need to be aligned.

- 'ES' indicates an extra seam allowance, where some projects require a wider seam allowance. Sew the seam to the end of the extra allowance. Fold under at the inner dashed line (if you are not joining to another piece).

- Generally, cut out the shapes *after* sewing, cutting about ¼in (6mm) outside of the sewn line (cutting by eye is fine).

- For some projects, you will need to add seam allowances to individual pieces – refer to the advice with the specific patterns.

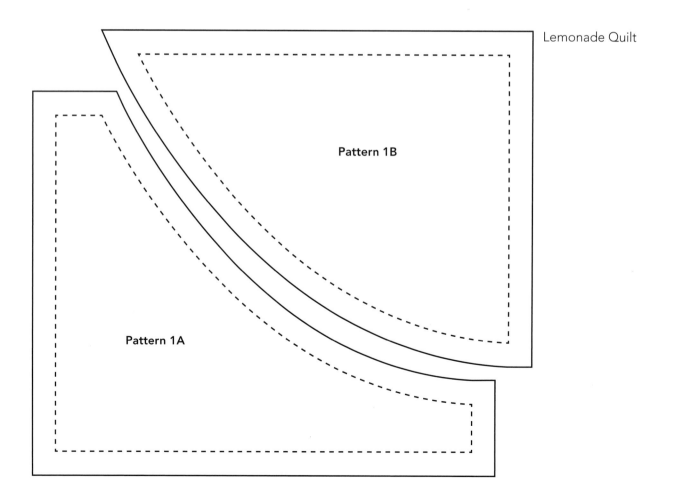

Lemonade Quilt

Pattern 1B

Pattern 1A

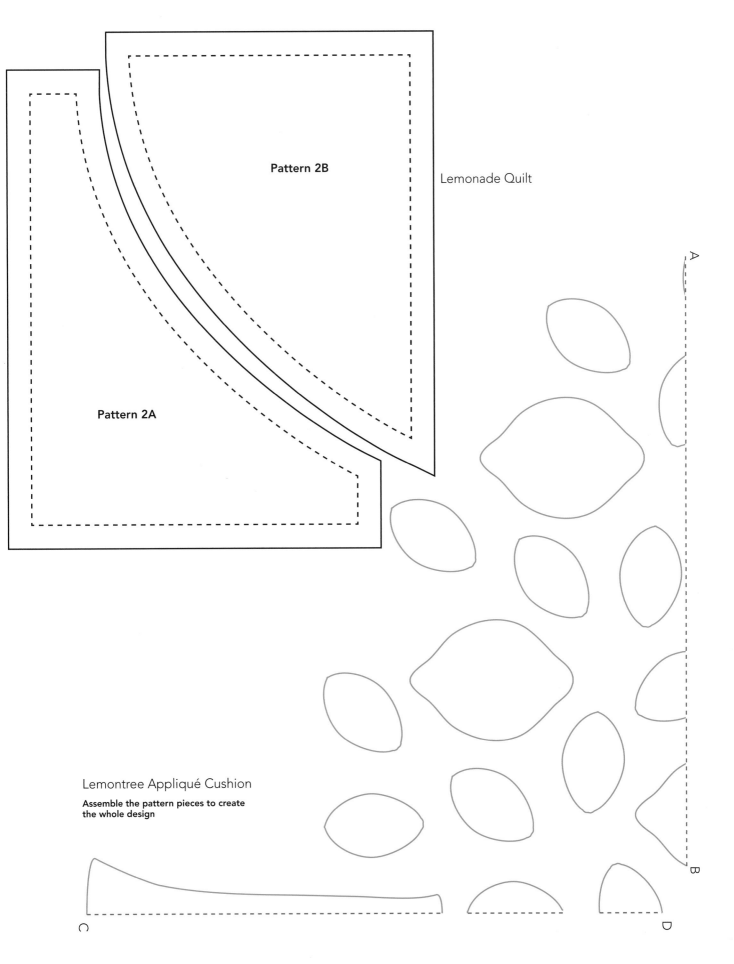

Pattern 2B

Lemonade Quilt

Pattern 2A

A

B

Lemontree Appliqué Cushion

Assemble the pattern pieces to create the whole design

C

D

Lemontree Appliqué Cushion
Assemble the pattern pieces to create the whole design

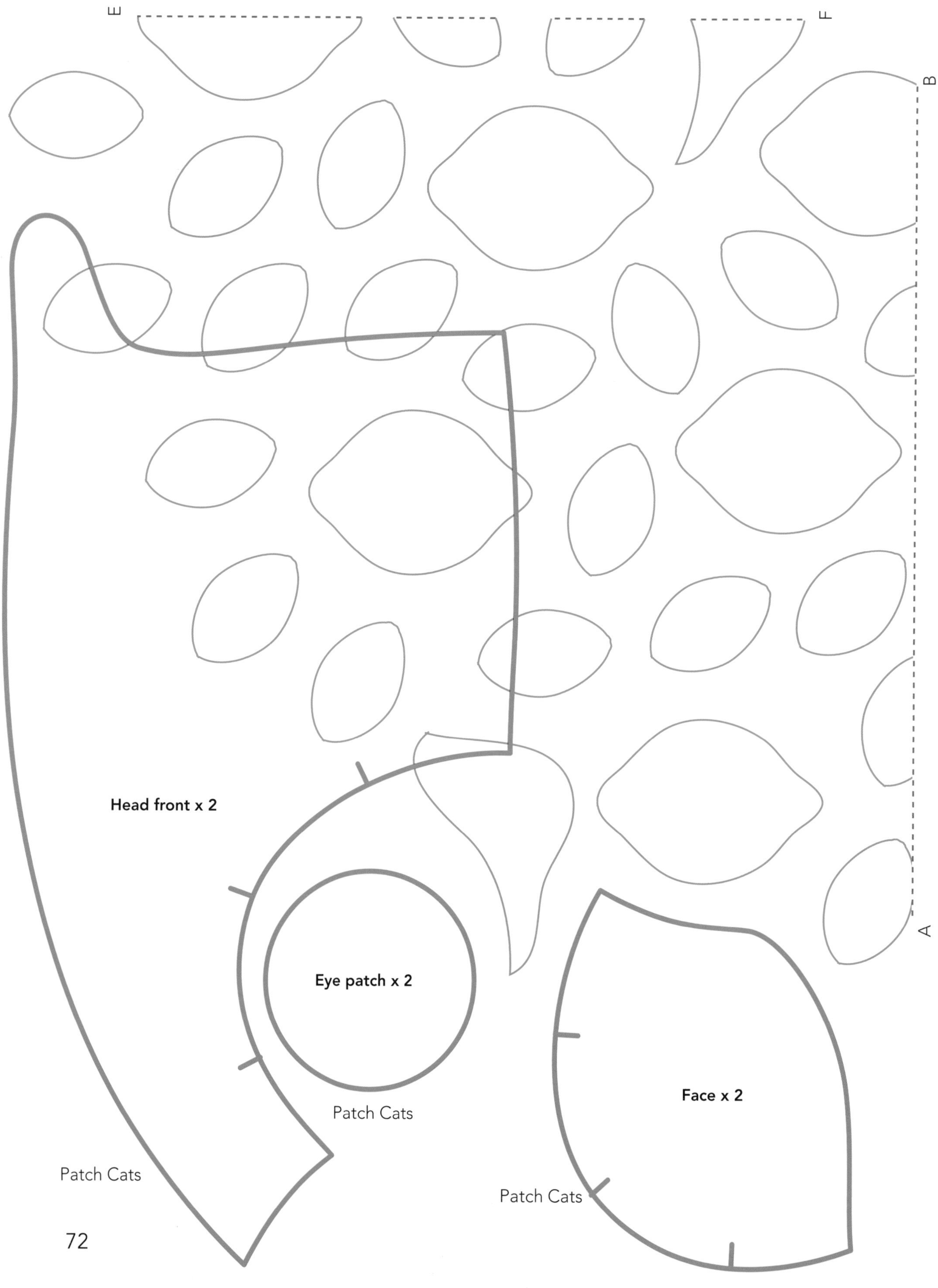

E

F

B

A

Head front x 2

Eye patch x 2

Patch Cats

Face x 2

Patch Cats

Patch Cats

Patch Cats

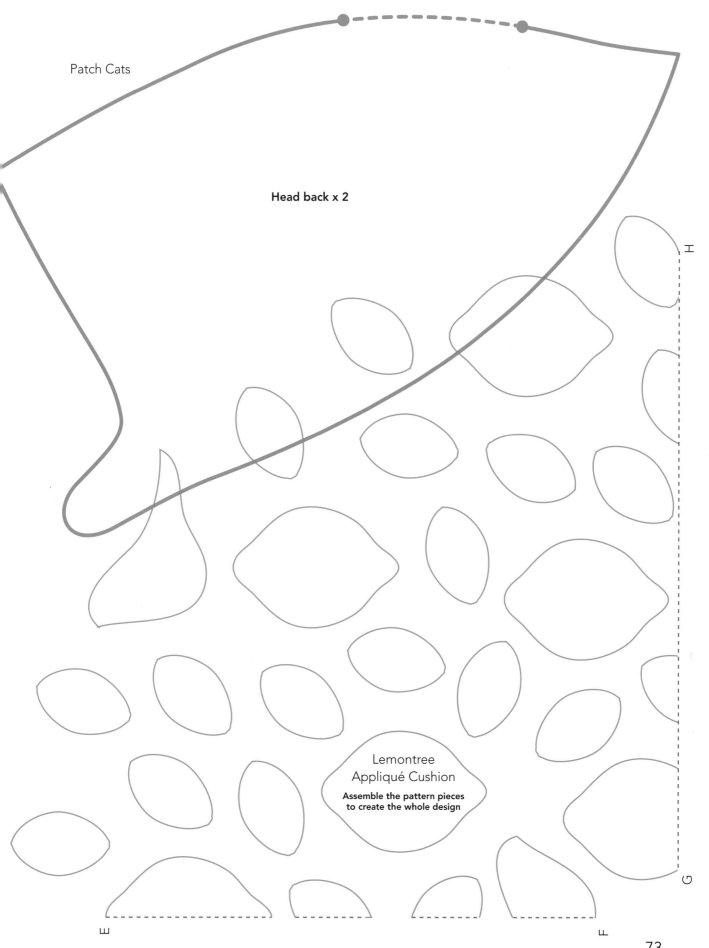

Patch Cats

Head back x 2

H

G

Lemontree
Appliqué Cushion

**Assemble the pattern pieces
to create the whole design**

E

F

73

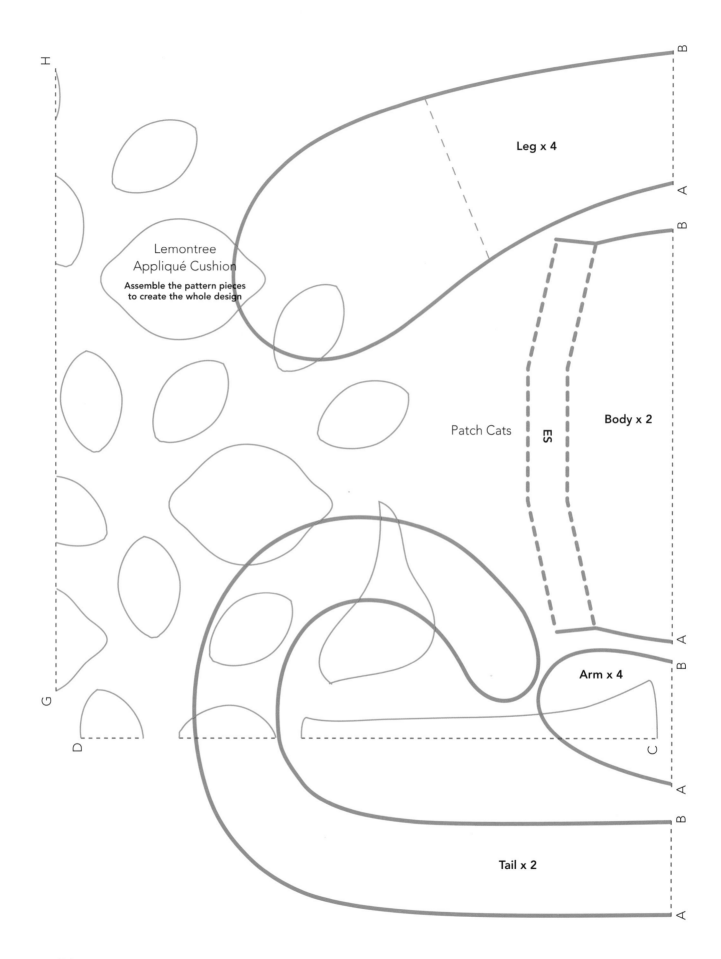

H

Leg x 4

B

A

Lemontree
Appliqué Cushion

**Assemble the pattern pieces
to create the whole design**

B

Patch Cats

ES

Body x 2

A

B

Arm x 4

G

D

C

A

B

Tail x 2

A

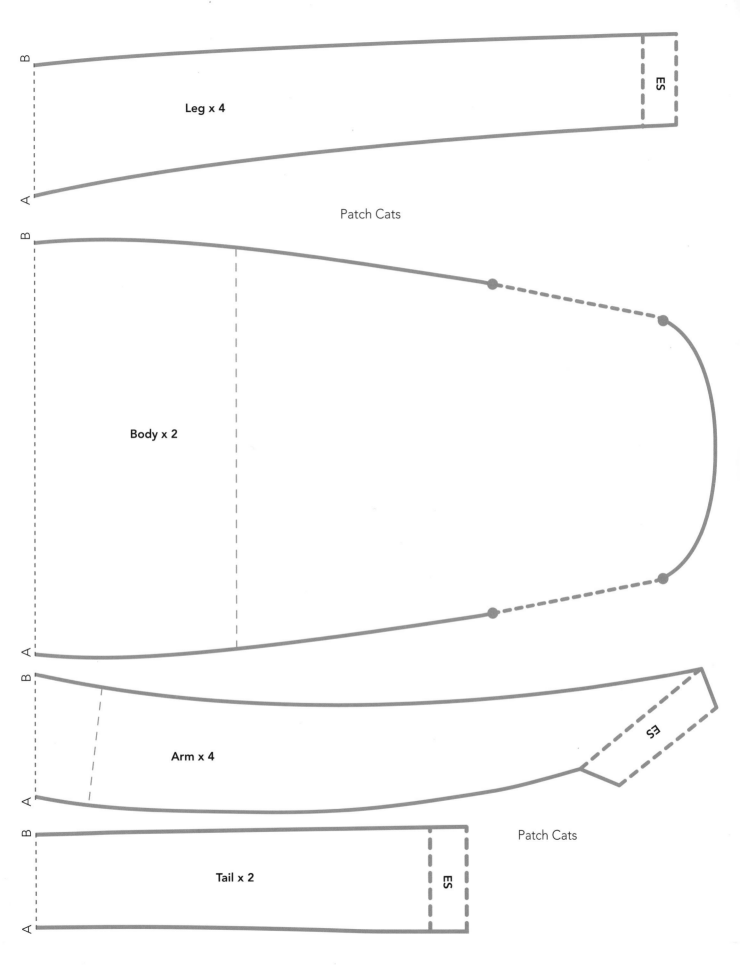

B

Leg x 4

ES

A

Patch Cats

B

Body x 2

A

B

Arm x 4

ES

A

B

Tail x 2

ES

A

Patch Cats

75

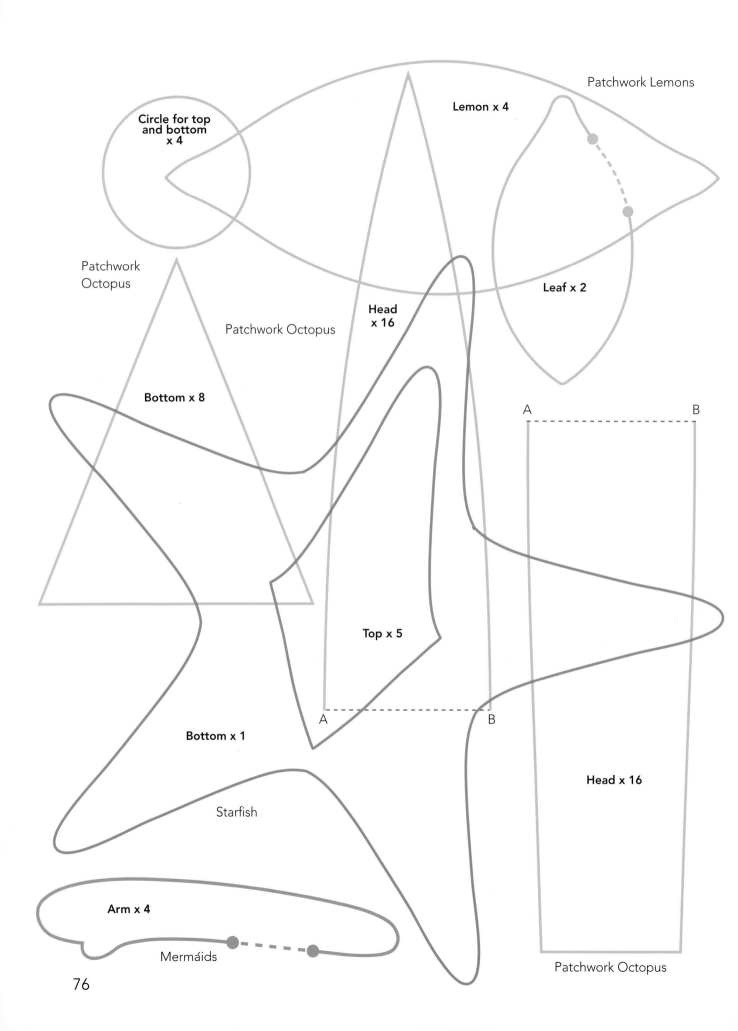

Patchwork Lemons

Circle for top and bottom x 4

Lemon x 4

Patchwork Octopus

Patchwork Octopus

Head x 16

Leaf x 2

Bottom x 8

A   B

Top x 5

A   B

Bottom x 1

Head x 16

Starfish

Arm x 4

Mermáids

Patchwork Octopus

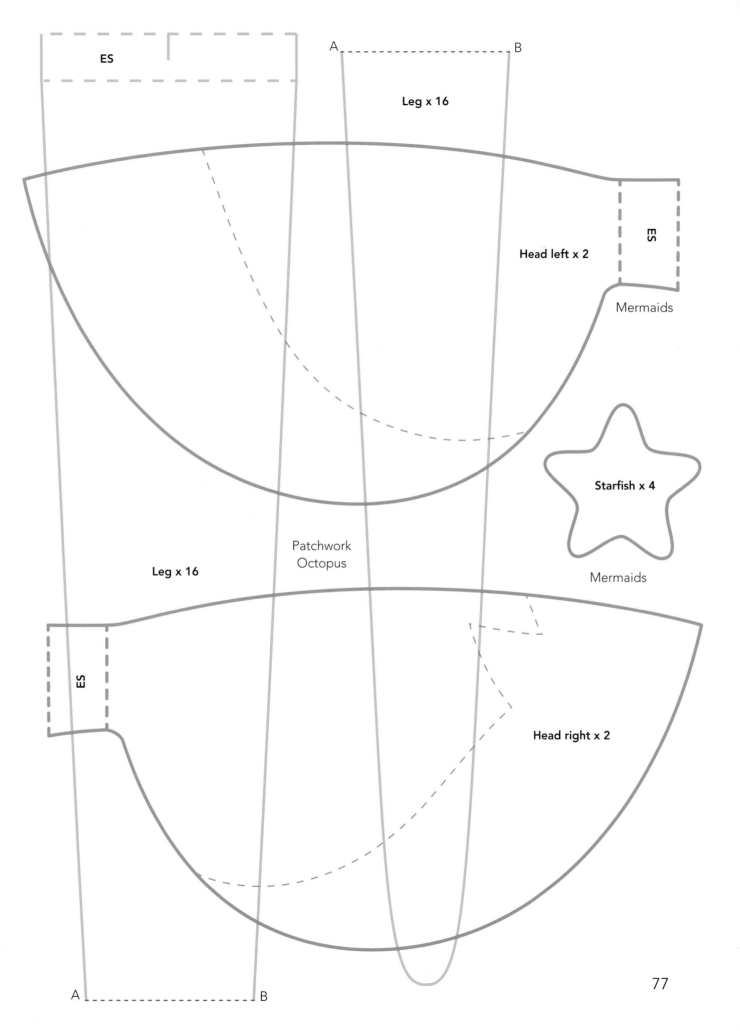

ES

A········B

Leg x 16

Head left x 2

ES

Mermaids

Starfish x 4

Mermaids

Patchwork
Octopus

Leg x 16

ES

Head right x 2

A········B

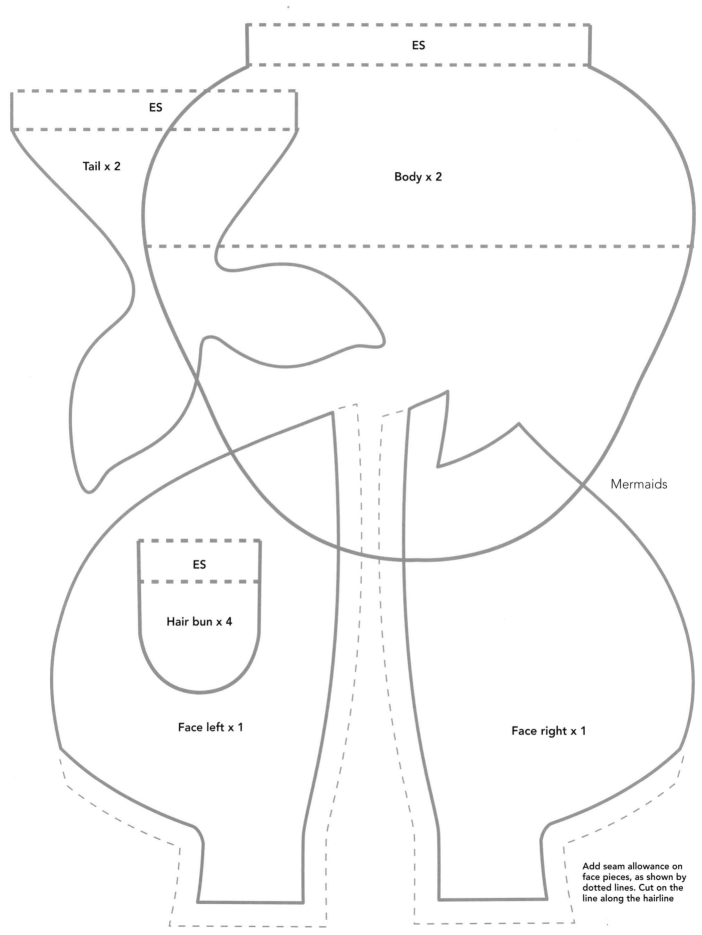

ES

ES

Tail x 2

Body x 2

Mermaids

ES

Hair bun x 4

Face left x 1

Face right x 1

Add seam allowance on face pieces, as shown by dotted lines. Cut on the line along the hairline

Tilda Fabrics

Tilda fabric is stocked in many stores worldwide. To find your nearest Tilda retailer, please search online or contact the Tilda wholesaler in your territory. For more information visit: www.tildafabrics.com.

EUROPE

Marienhoffgarden (Spain, Portugal, Germany, Italy, Holland, Belgium, Austria, Luxembourg, Switzerland and Denmark)
Industrivej 39, 8550 Ryomgaard, Denmark
Tel: +45 86395515
Email: mail@marienhoff.dk
www.marienhoff.dk

Industrial Textiles (Sweden, Norway, Finland, Iceland, Greenland and Germany)
Engholm Parkvej 1, 3450 Allerød, Denmark
Tel: +45 48 17 20 55
Email: mail@indutex.dk
www.indutex.dk

Groves (UK)
Eastern Bypass, Thame, OX9 3FU, UK
Tel: +44 (0) 1844 258 080
Email: sales@groves-banks.com
www.grovesltd.co.uk

Panduro Hobby (France)
BP 500, 74305 Cluses Cedex, France
Tel: +33 04 50 91 26 45
Email: info@panduro.fr
www.tildafrance.com

J. Pujol Maq Conf S.A.
(Spain and Portugal)
Pol. Ind. Les Pedreres, sector B, C/ Industria 5, 08390 Montgat, Barcelona, Spain
Tel: + 34 933 511 611
Email: jmpairo@jpujol.com
www.ideaspatch.com

NORTH AMERICA

Devonstone Square Inc. (USA)
19 West 34th St., Ste. 1018, New York, NY 10001, USA
Email: info@devonstonesquare.com
www.devonstonesquare.com

JN Harper (Canada and USA)
8335 Devonshire Road, Mont-Royal, Quebec H4P 2L1, Canada
Tel: +1 514 736 3000
Email: info@jnharper.com
www.jnharper.com

ASIA

Sing Mui Heng Ltd. (Singapore)
315 Outram Road, #05-09 Tan Boon Liat Building, Singapore 169074
Tel: +65 62219209
Email: enquiry@singmuiheng.com
www.smhcraft.com

Mianhexin Trading Co.,Ltd. (FlowerQuilt) (China Mainland)
Room 1001, New World Serviced Apartment, No.136, West Taige Road, Yixing City, Jiangsu Province, 214200 China
Tel: + 86 (510) 87926550
Email: flowerquilt@hotmail.com
www.flowerquilt.cn

Scanjap Incorporated (Japan, Hong Kong, Indonesia and Thailand)
Chiyoda-ku, Kudan-minami 3-7-12, Kudan Tamagawa Bld. 3F, 102-0074 Tokyo, Japan
Tel: +81 3 6272 9451
Email: yk@scanjap.com
www.tildajapan.com

THG International Ltd. (Thailand)
55/5-6 Soi Phaholyothin 11, Phaholyothin Rd., Samsen Nai, Phaya Thai, Bangkok 10400, Thailand

Quilt Friends (Malaysia)
C-G-33, G/Floor Block Camilia, 10 Boulevard, Sprint Highway, Kayu Ara PJU6A, 47400 Petaling Jaya, Selangor D.E., Malaysia
Tel: +60 377 293 110
Email: quilt_friends@outlook.com
www.quiltfriends.net

Long Teh Trading Co. Ltd. (Taiwan)
No. 71, Hebei W. St., Beitun District, Taichung City 40669, Taiwan
Tel: +886 4 2247 7711
Email: longteh.quilt@gmail.com
www.patchworklife.com.tw

M&S Solution (South Korea)
Gangnam B/D 7F, 217, Dosan-daero, Gangnam-gu, Seoul, South Korea
Tel: +82 (2) 3446 7650
Email: godsky0001@gmail.com

AUSTRALIA

Two Green Zebras
(Australia and New Zealand)
PO BOX 530, Tewantin, Queensland 4565, Australia
Tel: +61 (0) 2 9553 7201
Email: sales@twogreenzebras.com
www.twogreenzebras.com

AFRICA

Barrosa Trading Trust (Liefielove) (South Africa)
9D Kogel Street, Middelburg, Mpumalanga 1050, South Africa
Tel: +27 (0) 847 575 177
Email: liefielove11@gmail.com
www.liefielove.co.za

Index

A SEWANDSO BOOK
© F&W Media International, Ltd 2018

SewandSo is an imprint of F&W Media International, Ltd
Pynes Hill Court, Pynes Hill, Exeter, EX2 5AZ, UK

F&W Media International, Ltd is a subsidiary of F+W Media, Inc
10151 Carver Road, Suite #200, Blue Ash, OH 45242, USA

Text and Designs © Tone Finnanger 2018
Layout and Photography © F&W Media International, Ltd 2018

First published in the UK and USA in 2018

Tone Finnanger has asserted her right to be identified as author of this work in accordance with the Copyright, Designs and Patents Act, 1988.

All rights reserved. No part of this publication may be reproduced in any form or by any means, electronic or mechanical, by photocopying, recording or otherwise, without prior permission in writing from the publisher.

Readers are permitted to reproduce any of the patterns or designs in this book for their personal use and without the prior permission of the publisher. However, the designs in this book are copyright and must not be reproduced for resale.

The author and publisher have made every effort to ensure that all the instructions in the book are accurate and safe, and therefore cannot accept liability for any resulting injury, damage or loss to persons or property, however it may arise.

Names of manufacturers and product ranges are provided for the information of readers, with no intention to infringe copyright or trademarks.

A catalogue record for this book is available from the British Library.

ISBN-13: 978-1-4463-0702-1 paperback
SRN: R7470 paperback

ISBN-13: 978-1-4463-7661-4 PDF
SRN: R7609 PDF

ISBN-13: 978-1-4463-7662-1 EPUB
SRN: R7608 EPUB

Printed in the UK by Pureprint Group for:
F&W Media International, Ltd
Pynes Hill Court, Pynes Hill, Exeter, EX2 5AZ, UK

10 9 8 7 6 5 4 3

Content Director: Ame Verso
Managing Editor: Jeni Hennah
Project Editor: Lin Clements
Designer: Prudence Rogers
Seamstress: Ingun Eldøy
Stylist: Line Dammen
Photographer: Inger Marie Grini

F&W Media publishes high quality books on a wide range of subjects. For more great book ideas visit: www.sewandso.co.uk

Layout of the digital edition of this book may vary depending on reader hardware and display settings.